I LOVE THE SEASIDE

CONTENTS

5 - 11 ◆ **INTRO**
5 ◆ A WORD FROM US
6 ◆ HOW TO USE THIS GUIDE & PRICES
7 ◆ SURF SCHOOLS, SHOPS & SURF SPOTS
11 ◆ CHILE

12 - 33 ◆ **NORTE GRANDE**
12 ◆ MAP
13 - 19 ◆ IN AND AROUND ARICA
20 - 25 ◆ IN AND AROUND IQUIQUE
26 - 29 ◆ IN AND AROUND ANTOFAGASTA
30 - 33 ◆ SURF & SCHOOL RENTAL SHOP
34 - 39 ◆ SEASIDE LOCAL: LORENA FICA
41 ◆ YOGA POSE: BALANCING

44 - 65 ◆ **NORTE CHICO**
44 ◆ MAP
45 - 53 ◆ IN AND AROUND PORTOFINO TO BAHIA INGLESA
54 - 61 ◆ IN AND AROUND LA SERENA AND TOTORALILLO
62 - 65 ◆ SURF & SCHOOL RENTAL SHOP
67 ◆ YOGA POSE: STRETCHING THE SIDE BODY

72 - 123 ◆ **CENTRAL**
72 ◆ MAP
73 - 79 ◆ IN AND AROUND LOS MOLLES, ZAPALLAR AND MAITENCILLO
80 - 87 ◆ IN AND AROUND VALPARAÍSO AND VIÑA DEL MAR
88 - 93 ◆ IN AND AROUND ALGARROBO AND SANTO DOMINGO
94 - 101 ◆ IN AND AROUND MATANZAS AND PUERTECILLO

YOGA POSE: BACKBEND ◆ 105
IN AND AROUND PICHILEMU ◆ 106 - 115
SURF & SCHOOL RENTAL SHOP ◆ 116 - 123
SAVE THE WAVES ◆ 124 - 125
SURFER'S EAR ◆ 127
SEASIDE LOCAL: KRIS CABEZA ◆ 128 - 135
YOGA POSE: ◆ 137
FULL BODY STRETCH AND STRENGTHEN

SOUTH ◆ 140 - 177
MAP ◆ 140
IN AND AROUND VICHUQUÉN ◆ 141 - 145
IN AND AROUND CONSTITUCIÓN ◆ 146 -149
IN AND AROUND CURANIPE ◆ 150 - 155
YOGA POSE: RESTORATIVE POSE ◆ 157
IN AND AROUND ◆ 158 - 163
BUCHUPUREO AND COBQUECURA
IN AND AROUND ◆ 166 - 171
CONCEPCIÓN AND THE COAL COAST
SURF & SCHOOL RENTAL SHOP ◆ 172 - 177
YOGA POSE: BUILDING CONFIDENCE ◆ 181

NORTH PATAGONIA ◆ 184 - 209
MAP ◆ 184
IN AND AROUND VALDIVIA ◆ 185 - 193
IN AND AROUND PUCATRIHUE ◆ 194 - 199
IN AND AROUND ISLA GRANDE DE CHILOÉ ◆ 200 - 205
SURF & SCHOOL RENTAL SHOP ◆ 206 -209
SEASIDE LOCAL: VICTORIA ANSALDO ◆ 210 - 215
YOGA POSE: BALANCING ◆ 217
THERE'S MORE I LOVE THE SEASIDE! ◆ 220 - 221
THANK YOU & ABOUT US ◆ 222 - 223

A WORD FROM US

◆

So far, we've surf-and-travel-shared all we love along the European (surf) coast and a little beyond - Morocco! Then we started preparing to spread our salty wings and see what's what and who's who overseas. To be sure of giving you the low-down with all the best local knowledge, we expanded our tiny team for this Chile edition to include explorers Marte and Vicente.

The sum of a local and a tourist, the perfect fit.

Vicente Gracia, born and raised in Chile, and Dutchie Marte Louwes both love to explore, discover new perspectives and insights, learn new languages and customs, and try different foods. Being the sum of a local and a tourist they made the perfect fit to carefully choose the people, places and stories for this book. They've a passion for Chile, a passion to show the world this amazing country, nature, and coastline. After traveling and catching waves all over the world, they're comfortable saying that the magic you find in Chile, you won't easily find anywhere else.

*The goal is to connect the local community with
a greater like-minded community.*

AND A WORD FROM THEM

◆

"There is so much raw beauty out there that needs to be seen. The endless coast of Chile and the constantly changing views, landscapes and climates. We were pleasantly surprised by the awesome coffee places, vegan-friendly food bowls and beautiful beach bars we discovered along the way. Our dream is to share with you our love for Chile's people, waves, coastline, food and travel. To connect the local community with a greater like-minded community. Abrazos, Marte and Vicente"

HOW TO USE THIS GUIDE

♦

In this edition we guide you down Chile's coast, from north to south. Obviously, we expect that you'll travel your own route; dropping in and out wherever suits, using a chapter, skipping to your next destination, or curled up at home on the sofa, flicking through the guide and dreaming of adventures to come. Our aim, and greatest hope, is to guide you along and inspire you on your journey, whether you're a surfer, a seaside lover or simply a traveler who admires the great outdoors!

We don't stop at each and every spot, or list every place we've been, but if you follow the coast from one area to the next, you'll find each place we pinpoint is a central location from which you can go and explore. It's essentially the ocean that takes the place of your compass. Any not-so-seaside things we recommend for you to discover are within a day's drive from the seaside.

PRICES

♦

Due to seasonal price changes, especially for hotels and campsites, we've chosen to use symbols which give you an indication of price ranges. Note that it's all relative, the ♦$♦ or ♦$$♦ range suit Chile standards.

♦

♦$♦ *Cheap as chips*
♦$$♦ *Pretty reasonable*
♦$$$♦ *Affordable treat*
♦$$$$♦ *Luxurious extravagance*

♦

SURF SCHOOLS AND SHOPS

◆

Big thing in this guide, without a doubt. The schools and shops mentioned within are either approved and loved by us, or recommended by folk we trust. Those that we don't mention: it doesn't mean they're inferior, malfunctioning or what-not. Certainly not. In some surfing areas there are so many, with so little difference between them, that in those areas we chose those we feel offer special character or atmosphere, that add a twist to the definition of surf shop. In the areas where schools and shops are scarce, we mention any in the area, because they can be useful if in need of wax, leash, repair, etc.

SURF SPOTS

◆

On their travels along the coast of Chile, our researchers met so many friendly locals, surfers and saltwater addicts. Most of them were happy to share waves and even take them out to their favorite local - but sometimes secret - surf spot. We respect that, and them, and therefore try to avoid misusing those warm and welcoming gestures by not mentioning all spots. While we only list the well-known, that doesn't mean there aren't many more spots to discover for yourself. So, since we're huge fans of exploring and meeting new people to learn, share, and make friends, we encourage you to do a little exploring yourself, with that same respect in mind. We sincerely hope you understand our choice.

◆

Not all who wander are lost.

◆

Welcome to Chile.

@ yeticampers

Welcome to YETI CAMPERS.

www.yeticampers.com

CHILE

Yay, Chile - 6,435 kilometers of coastline! Like a slender supermodel with endless legs, Chile is long and narrow. There are many natural extremes to the geography of the country; you could be stargazing in the arid desert in the Far North one day, then traveling through fertile wine valleys in Central Chile. Soon after, you can drive through the Lake District's ancient forests to the Chiloé archipelago in Northern Patagonia… there's always something new and totally different just around the bend.

TRAVEL

Traveling to Chile means traveling to one of the safest countries in South America. You'll soon discover (especially if you fly in via modern Santiago with its well-kept highways) that it's easy too. Drives are long-distance - the country measures over 4000 kms from north to south, after all - but mainly along good roads. Some small reach-the-beach roads, however, can be bumpy, so a 4-wheel drive can help you get to places you might otherwise need to bypass.

Marte and Vicente traveled in both a rental car, with an easy-to-use and smart roof tent, from TRIBU (w. carpastribu.cl), and in one of the well-equipped 4x4 campervans from YETI CAMPERS (w. yeticampers.com). They highly recommend both!

SURF

Surf spots are so numerous that anyone ticking off breaks will have arms like Arnold before they're halfway. Chile's the land of powerful lefts, cold water and unspoiled, awe-inspiring backdrops. While some places have been on the surf radar for a while now, and can be as crowded as any popular break around the globe, there are also many remote, unknown and pristine spots.

We're not here to disclose any secret spots, but to inspire you to connect and seek advice from the local surf communities, share smiles not locations, and respect the land, culture and line-ups.

IN & AROUND ARICA

The most northerly city of Chile, capital of the region Arica y Parinacota, is considered the door to the Altiplano - the plateau of South America - and so you'll find an interesting combination of cultures and traditions here, with a long history of Chilean Altiplano peoples mixing with those of Peru and Bolivia. Called the 'City of the Eternal Spring' due to its year-round good weather, it's a hop-in-hop-out transition stop for many travelers passing through on the way in and out of Peru. Besides its cool desert city backpacker vibe and lively nightlife, Arica has great surf options along its coastline of brown sugar beaches, and a strong surf community. Among the world class waves on offer, it's home to the famous 'El Gringo' - known as the Chilean Pipeline - and hosts many well-known competitions.

Also famous for the Chinchorro Mummies (more about the Mummies below in case you don't know), the feeling of being on ancient lands is inescapable, with small villages and towns holding onto their heritage, characterized by local architecture that pre-dates the arrival of the Spanish conquistadors. The Parinacota Route leads you through the heritage towns of San Miguel de Azapa, Putre, Parinacota, Socorama, Belen, Codpa and Poconchile, some of the towns hundreds of years old and characterized by their churches and whitewashed buildings. In the fertile Lluta Valley, surrounded by the Atacama desert, you can see imposing cactus, the enormous geoglyphs of El Gigante and Las Colcas, and in the Lauca National Park, find one of the highest lakes in the world - Chungará Lake. Fancy finding out whether coldwater swimming cures altitude sickness? Let us know!

TO DO

◆

Held every summer in January or February, the **Carnaval Andino Internacional con la Fuerza del Sol Inti Ch'amampi** (**1**) promotes and celebrates Andean culture through dance and music. Con La Fuerza, meaning With the Force of the Sun, is an apt name for such a dusty dry climate. Don't forget your sunscreen and plenty of water if you're planning to join the thousands of dancers and musicians who travel from far and wide to the 3-day long celebration - one of the largest and most important carnivals in South America. There's an entrance fee for some music events, but most of the festival areas are free to roam, dance and admire.

a. Historic center of Arica
fb. Carnaval con la Fuerza del Sol

Walk around the narrow streets of the **Centro Histórico** (**2**) to get a glimpse of the heritage and history of the city. In less than 15 blocks, you'll see

valuable heritage and buildings. The center has the typical Spanish colonial layout, with the main square, Plaza Fundacional, and the Catedral San Marcos - a gothic-style church designed by none other than Parisian engineer Alexandre Gustave Eiffel in 1876, before his success with the Eiffel Tower. Wander freely and admire at any time of year.

a. San Marcos 251, Arica

For a panoramic vista, a **hike up Morro de Arica** (**3**) will give you a superb view of the city, desert and ocean, with the Andes in the distance. It's a huge sandy landmark that can't be missed, so no directions needed - about 15 minutes' walk to the top.

On your way up you'll find the site of the famously discovered Chinchorro Mummies, and Museo Histórico y de Armas at the top, where you can learn some about the War of the Pacific which took place in 1880. The Morro's accessible all year, museo open all year with a small entrance fee.

a. Morro de Arica, Arica

The Chinchorro Mummies are the mummified remains of the Chinchorro peoples who inhabited the lands thousands of years before us. They're also the oldest examples ever found of intentionally preserved human bodies, with the earliest of them dated at around 5050 BC. At least 2000 years older than the first Egyptian mummies.

If you're curious to get a sneak-peek at the collection of mummies on display in Arica, you'll see just that at Museo Sitio Colón 10, on the way up El Morro. It's a tiny museum and gets mixed reviews, so don't expect a long tour - just a number of mummies under a glass-bottomed building. If you want to learn some about the Chinchorro culture and history, you can find plenty more to see and get in-depth information in the **Museo de Arqueologico San Miguel de Azapa (4)**, just half an hour's drive away. Open all year.

a. Cristóbal Colón 10, Morro de Arica, Arica / Camino Azapa 12, Arica
t. +56 58 220 5041 (Colón) / 58 220 5041 (Azapa)
fb. Museo Colon 100, Cultura Chinchorro
w. museouta.cl

Whether you're starting or ending your trip here, passing through on the way to Perú or the other way around, it's the perfect time to indulge yourself with a sauna, jacuzzi, massage or wellness treatment at **Hotel and Spa Las Taguas (5)**. Open all year.

a. Edmundo Perez Zujovic 280, Arica
t. +56 9 6568 9768
i. lastaguas.spa

Find more historical artifacts, a paradisical fishing cove and a small trekking trail about an hour's drive south of Arica in the tiny village of **Caleta Vitor (6)**. Well worth a day trip to explore and enjoy the delights, from the mirador offering a grand view to the cave at the south end of the beach, where original cave paintings can be seen, along with textile scraps including plant fiber mats, and Chinchorro human remains nearby. In addition, find some slightly more modern (and less mummified) cannons left behind by the Chilean Navy. Accessible all year.

a. Caleta Vitor, Arica

EAT/DRINK/HANG OUT
♦

At the top of Playa Las Machas, **Océano Surf & Café (7)** is the don't-miss-out-must-coffee-and-eat-stop of Arica. Run by professional bodyboarder Savitri and her partner, professional surfer Alberto, find healthy wholesome homemade tasty goodness with some gentle influences from India on the menu, with plenty veggie/vegan options and even Ayurveda-eats.

Alongside the relaxed pet-friendly wooden terrace, you can watch people working out on the neighbouring exercise bars and feel even healthier about yourself. Or use them too for a feeling-fit double-whammy. You can also get surf rentals here. Open all year. ♦$$♦ ♦$$$♦

a. Avenida Eilat, Playa Las Machas, Arica
i. oceano_surfcafe

Another eat at the beach option, **Akua Natural Café (8)** also offers plenty of healthy options and great coffee. Find all kinds of bowls; Acai, Chai, Pitaya and more, veggie and vegan options, and happy pets hanging out feeling most welcome. They also have a surf school (Escuela de Surf Akua) and offer yoga classes. Open all year.
♦$$♦ ♦$$$♦

a. Ingeniero Raúl Pey Casado 3300, Arica
t. +56 9 5324 6694
i. akuanaturalcafe

In between the two superfoods stops above, **Rider Land (9)** serve up some tasty alternative fishy dishes, including sandwiches, fish crackling and ceviche, as well as empanadas. They also work together with Aloha Sushi to bring fresh sushi to the beachfront of Playa Las Machas. Seasonal opening.
♦$$♦ ♦$$$♦

a. Ingeniero Raúl Pey Casado 3348, Arica
i. riderland.arica

One of the best places to go for a good brekkie, **La Bicicleta Arica (10)** is located in town and opens early (8am), eager to delight with excellent coffees and natural juices, and a fine breakfast, brunch and lunch menu. Founded by two friends,

one local from Arica, the other from Santiago, they named their café La Bicicleta because they're super-keen to promote the two-wheels mode of transport in this very bike-friendly city. Open all year. ♦$$♦ ♦$$$♦

a. Chacabuco 340 Local 53, Arica
t. +56 9 6656 6913
fb. La Bicicleta Arica

Restaurant-bakery-eco-store **Eco Centro Arica (11)** is one of your best healthy and vegan options in town. Owned and run by a Nortina (from the north) veggie-loving family, they've a menu full of tempting deliciousness, everything-friendly bulk goods in the eco store, and also offer community services, including vegetarian cooking and organic gardening workshops, talks on spirituality and health, and offer yoga classes too. Check in and check it out. Open all year. ♦$$♦

a. 18 de Septiembre 2318, Arica
t. +56 58 224 7077
fb. ecocentroarica

We're not trying to ram plant-based foods down you, promise! It just so happens that there's a heap of choice in vegan cuisine within Arica's enviro-conscious community. **Togapop (12)** offers a 'Healthy and Conscious Rotisserie' selection of vegan dishes designed in a contemporary style, with a dash of Argentine innovation and a drizzle of flair. Open all year. ♦$$♦

a. San Marco 510, Arica
t. +56 9 3272 7582
fb. togapop

SHOP
♦

Shop for produce and products grown/made in the region, as well as some originating from Peru and Bolivia, at the Sunday market - **Feria Dominical (13)**. The highlights are the crafts and unique handmade goods, or maybe the Andean sweets on offer, such as Chumbeques, Alfajores de Pica and Pululus, among many more. If you've any cash left after buying and trying a few of each sugary treat on display, you can also get basic supplies and essentials like cosmetics, and find second-hand clothes, books, bits and bobs. Aim to arrive early if you can; there are bargains to be had. Open all day every Sunday, all year.

a. Chacabuco Street, Arica

Founded in 1979 thanks to the initiative of artisan José Naranjo Meneses, **Poblado Artesanal (14)** was created to concentrate artisanal activity and provide an attraction for visitors. Built with adobe construction techniques, as a replica of highland town Parinacota, the village provides homes and workshops for up to 12 artisans with trades in crafts such as ceramics, textiles, leather, candle-making, brewing beer and goldsmithing. There's also a central plaza in which workshops, concerts and cultural events are held. Open all year.

a. Hualles 2825, Arica
t. +56 58 238 6628
w. pobladoartesanal.cl

SLEEP

◆

Phuqata Surf Camp (15) is a multicultural hostel-style sociable stay with good vibes, private rooms and shared bunk rooms available, a big pool and plenty hangout space to mingle with your fellow guests. Run by six-times national surf champion Lorena Fica and her family, they welcome you to join get-togethers,

from BBQs to musical/games nights and shared meals - you're part of the family from the moment you arrive. The place is covered with vibrant wall paintings and has safe parking for your ride (which you'll need to get into town/to the beach as it's a 10-minute drive to the nearest playa). Open all year. ◆$$◆

a. Isabel Riquelme 43, Villa Frontera, Arica
t. +56 9 9505 8390
w. phuqatahostel.com

Willka Kuti Hostel (16) is a classic clean and friendly stop for backpackers, colorful and perfectly set up to party, right in front of the beach. Choose from shared dormitory or private room and make yourself at home in the communal social areas, as can your pet(s) - they're welcome here too. Open all year. ◆$◆ ◆$$◆

a. Brasilia 2465, Arica
t. +56 9 8668 3194
fb. Willka Kuti Backpackers

With more of a traditional hotel, family-stay kinda feeling, **Panamericana Hotel Arica (17)** sits on the south edge of the city (about a 15-minute walk from the center) in front of the El Buey wave and fairly close to Alacran Peninsula, where you can find a few famous waves. The story goes (from

staff at the hotel) that when Kelly Slater stayed here for competitions he'd paddle from the hotel along to El Gringo, while the rest of the compe-

titors walked. Double, twin and family rooms are available, they've a nice-looking bar and restaurant and a beachside outdoor swimming pool, and a super view from the terrace. Open all year. ◆$$$◆

a. Avenida Comandante San Martín 599, Arica
t. +56 58 225 4540
w. panamericanahoteles.cl/arica

A short skip along the promenade from the Panamericana, **Hotel Apacheta (18)** has a striking appearance, built completely from wood, metal and glass to meet sustainable design criteria. The name Apacheta comes from the Quechua word apachita, meaning a pile of stones placed one on top of the other, forming a monolith. These were used by indigenous travelers on the Inca Trail as offerings to Pachamama (Mother Earth) and Apus (God of the Mountains) in exchange for protection. They've 18 stylish rooms, all with an ocean view and private bathroom, and one with disabled access. Open all year. ◆$$$◆

a. Avenida Comandante San Martín 661, Arica
t. +56 58 252 0150
w. hotelapacheta.com

IN AND AROUND IQUIQUE

•

Port city and capital of the Tarapacá Region, the name Iquique comes from the indigenous Aymara name Iki Iki, meaning Place of Dreams, Place of Rest. Well, if you're into what's on offer round here, it's all that and a bit more. Once big and busy for saltpeter mining, Iquique's now a hotspot for sea and sky sports, with numerous quality surf breaks accessible from the beachfront boardwalk and consistently clear skies, powerful air currents and high-altitude dunes and ravines creating the ideal setting for paragliders. If you're a fan of trekking an arid desert landscape scattered with geoglyphs to work up a sweat then refreshing yourself in the cold sea - like an outdoor sauna-to-plunge-pool paradise, for free! - and duty-free shopping, then all's golden along this crescent-shaped coastline.

Within the city, if shopping in La Zofri (the duty-free mall) doesn't appeal and you're seeking more Olde Worlde quaint and quirky, wander the old-school cobbled boulevard 'Paseo Baquedano', hop on a tram from the Arturo Prat Monument to Plaza Arturo Prat, and check out historical beauties like rows of heritage houses, the Torre del Reloj (clock tower) and the Municipal Theater. Many of the grand designs were built during the era of reaping riches from the saltpeter industry. The coast, however, is a natural-design-playas-aplenty place; from the well-known beaches Cavancha, Brava and Huaiquique to the less built-up-around spots like Punta Gruesa, Playa Blanca and (if you're inclined to escape the city vibe and aren't put off by a little journey) Playa Ike-Ike, an hour or two's drive south.

TO DO

◆

Don't miss **Fiesta La Tirana (19)** if you're in or around Iquique in July. Unless you're overwhelmed by a 200-odd-thousand-strong crowd of people dancing in masks and having the biggest fun. Held in the tiny desert town of La Tirana, the week-long fiesta's held in honor of the Virgen del Carmen and is one of the most popular, most colorful multicultural celebrations in Chile. Free entry.

a. Pampa del Tamarugal, La Tirana, Iquique

Get a little knowledge of the region's culture and history at the **Museo Regional (20)**. It's also another opportunity to see some Chinchorro Mummies if you skipped/are skipping the northerly neighbor city of Arica (or didn't pop in for a peek at the mummified remains from the ancient civilization while you were there). Formerly a courthouse, the construction now replicates a traditional Altiplano village. Open all year, free entry.

a. Baquedano 951, Iquique
t. +56 57 254 4719
fb. Museo Regional de Iquique

Get your Hatha flow, Animal flow, or restorative yoga session on the go with surfer-yogi Javier at **Casa Ananda (21)**. Classes are held in the studio at the house, located about a block from the beach. Their sister project, Ananda Surf Lab, offers comprehensive surf training for all levels and yoga-surf classes are available too - what a combo! Open all year.

a. Obispo Labbe 1589, Iquique
t. +56 9 5732 1687
fb. Ananda Yoga Iquique

If the surf's not up to par or you fancy something dry to ride, howzzabout carving up the giant dune that overlooks the city with two-time sandboard world champion Jose Martinez of **Sandboard Iquique (22)**. Lessons and tours of the natural park are on offer, the full package includes transportation, equipment, professional instruction and pictures/videos. The fine golden-white sand dune, Cerro El Dragón, rises 230 meters above sea level and is four kilometers long, so could well be the longest ride of your life. Open all year.

a. Los Algarrobos 3786, Iquique
t. +56 9 8371 5040
fb. Sandboard Iquique

According to the experts, the average number of days that the wind and weather don't work in favor of paragliding around here is 7 days a year. So, as long as you picked one of the other 358 days, you should be good to go. Experienced and certificated instructor Cristian at **Oasisfly (23)** speaks good English and can arrange everything for you to take to the skies. Open all year.

a. Jose Francisco Vergara 2938, Iquique
t. +56 9 9077 4362
w. oasisfly.cl

Find **Skatepark Iquique (24)** overlooking the bay of Playa Brava. The concrete park's perhaps designed mostly with BMX in mind, but has plenty of lines and is free for all, and open all year.

a. Avenida Arturo Prat Chacón 9, Iquique

Traveling south on the Panamericana Norte, about an hour's drive inland from Iquique, find protected nature area **Reserva Nacional Pampa del Tamarugal (25)** covering over a thousand square kilometers. There are three sectors in the reserve: Zapiga, Bosque Nativo de La Tirana, and Pintados. There's a surprising amount of woodland despite the bosque being so deep in the desert - the area was replanted in the 1980s with native tamarugo, white carob, chulki and fortune trees (among others) after coming close to depletion due to the demand for its excellent quality wood - but very little wildlife beyond the odd fox, some reptiles, rodents and birds. The Geoglifos de Pintados is the main attraction; over 2 kilometers of symbols made from stone on the slopes, depicting men, animals and geometric figures. Created between 700 and 1500 AD, the symbols are thought to have been guides to help caravans of travelers find water sources and routes, and to celebrate rituals. The town of Pintados itself is derelict, with nothing but a disused rail station, an artisanal store and 1 inhabitant. Entry's free for the reserve and Environmental Education Center, there's a small fee to enter the Museo Sitio to see the geoglyphs. There are also 4 small camping sites with basic facilities - find the main office in direction of Pozo Almonte if you want to check in for an overnight stay. Open all year.

a. Reserva Nacional Pampa del Tamarugal, La Tirana - Pintados, Pozo Almonte
t. +56 9 8595 3756
w. conaf.cl/parques/reserva-nacional-pampa-del-tamarugal

EAT/DRINK/HANG OUT
◆

Choose from typical South American dishes and seafood or opt for a taste of Thailand at **El Tercer Ojito (26)**. The laidback pet-friendly restaurant has a nice 'patio Andaluz-style' garden with lots of greenery and serves up good, fresh food with healthy options and plenty on the menu for veggies. Open all year. ◆$$◆

a. Patricio Lynch 1420, Iquique
t. +56 9 7432 6167
i. eltercerojito

Get your quick-fix post-surf (sandwich or homemade burger and fries) feed at **La Mayor Sandwichería (27)** and choose from an impressive variety of beers (locals and imports) to go with it. Going for simplicity, sandwich and beer, can't go wrong. Open all year. ◆$◆

a. Céspedes y González 717, Iquique
t. +56 9 8919 7515
fb. La Mayor Sandwicheria

Right next to Backpacker's Hostel, you'll find **Backpacker's Café (28)** where you'll likely meet a number of - you got it… backpackers! The popular little coffee corner has a small terrace and is a short walk from Playa Cavancha beach. Offering coffees, juices, sandwiches and bakes, you can also rent a bike or book activities and excursions from here. Open all year.
◆$$◆

a. Amunátegui 2075, Iquique
t. +56 9 6172 6788
fb. Backpacker's Hostel Iquique

If you're after a bit of a change and some fancier than usual food, **La Mulata (29)** serves up Peruvian and Nikkei fusion (Peruana-Japonesa) flavors along with some cocktails we love to recommend - take the Pisco Sour challenge and see whether you prefer the Chilean or Peruvian version. If you wobble off and wake up with a hangover you can always come back the following day for a Ceviche Carretillero; the best 'levanta muertos' (waken the dead) cure we ever tried. Portions are generous, the dishes are beautifully presented, and you've a little peek of a view over Playa Cavancha. Open all year. ◆$$◆ ◆$$$◆

a. Avenida Arturo Prat Chacón 902, Iquique
t. +56 9 4037 9770
w. lamulata.cl

Get set for another change in flavor and a full-on gastronomic experience in the form of a Mediterranean-style tasting series. The succession of 'slow food' dishes can be enjoyed on the bougainvillea-draped patio at **Santorini Restobar (30)**, where they embrace the Greek concept of estía - sharing around good food, seating yourself well in the present moment. Open all year. ◆$$$◆

a. Avenida Luis Emilio Recabarren 2808, Iquique
t. +56 57 222 5392
w. santorinirestobar.cl

If you haven't worn your fancy pants yet and have a mood for dressing up nice for a night out, best unpack them for your seaview dinner at **Chiringuito Cavancha (31)**. Their menu blends 'the flavors of our coast with everything endemic to our desert' accompanied by select wines and premium cocktails. Open all year. ◆$$$◆

a. Capitán Roberto Perez 250, Iquique
t. +56 9 5908 2258
w. chiringuitocavancha.cl

Sushi, ceviche, urban vibes and pisco sour. We could use a lot more words, but these pointers sum up what to expect at lavish sushi bar **Otaku (32)**. Open all year. ◆$$$◆

a. Capitán Roberto Perez 2791, Iquique
t. +56 57 243 4168
fb. Otaku Sushibar Peninsula

SHOP
◆

Stock up on the traditional sweets of Iquique at **Chumbeque M.koo (33)**. Find different flavors of Chumbeque (mango, guayaba, manjar and many others) along with cheesecakes and chocolate cakes and all the slabs of delight you ever dreamt of. The kind owner of the shop will be proud to serve you lots of local sweetness. Open all year.

a. Eleuterio Ramirez 949, Iquique
t. +56 9 9764 8168
fb. Chumbeques M.KOO

The 'healthy little market' **Mercadito Saludable** (**34**) is right in front of the beach and despite its cute size has a whole lot of vegan, keto, organic, gluten-free, medicinal infusion, coffee, and sugar-free staples that you can buy in bulk if you need to stock your camper cupboards. Open all year.

a. Avenida Arturo Prat Chacón 1724
t. +56 9 9984 2305
fb. Mercadito Saludable Iquique

SLEEP
♦

Backpacker's Hostel Iquique (**35**) is owned by surfer Vinco, who will welcome you with open arms, light the grill and hang out with you and the other guests. The funky hostel's a favorite stop for backpackers and is within walking distance of Playa Cavancha, so you can put on your suit and walk to the nearest break with no commute. Find inside; shared social areas, including a netflixnchillout section, kitchen, games - ping pong and pool tables and a buzzy fun atmosphere. Open all year. ♦$♦ ♦$$♦ .

a. Amunátegui 2075, Iquique
t. +56 9 6172 6788
fb. Backpacker's Hostel Iquique

Easygoing **Aotea Hostel Iquique** (**36**) is a relaxed stay with comfy rooms in a great location - just a short wander to the beach or into the city. Common areas and kitchen are spacious for mingling, as are the garden, BBQ area and swimming pool, and the man behind the name is (not so surprisingly) from the great green island of New Zealand.
Open all year. ♦$♦ ♦$$♦

a. Manuel Rodriguez 745, Iquique
t. +56 57 272 9578
fb. Aoteas Hostel Iquique

Located just 100 meters from Playa Cavancha and right next to a lively bar is **Hostal El Bajo** (**37**). Inside, find small but clean private and shared rooms (16 beds in total), and a common seating area with a small cafeteria-kiosk where they serve really good coffee. Rental bikes are available and owner Tito can also sort out any surf lessons or rental equipment you need. Open all year. ♦$$♦

a. Obispo Labbé 1659, Iquique
t. +56 9 6831 3028
fb. Hostel El Bajo

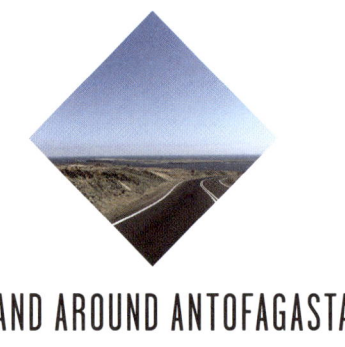

IN AND AROUND ANTOFAGASTA

The Antofagasta region offers vast arid desert land combined with a few surprisingly busy city ports along its coastline. Drive away from the surrounds of the cities and find yourself very quickly in the middle of a big dry nowhere. What? Drive as far inland as the higher altitudes of San Pedro de Atacama if you dare detach yourself from the ocean for a bit. Rest assured; the otherworldly surroundings of this little desert oasis with geysers, salt lakes and moon-like valleys will make up for the 3-4-hour drive. There are hostels, restaurants and adventures aplenty to choose from before your F(ear) O(f) M(issing) S(urf) surfaces again and you head back to sea.

Surf tourism hasn't developed much in this area yet - especially compared to the northern neighbours of Iquique and Arica - but if you're keen to travel the entire coast you'll find enough spots here to explore (even more if you have a reliable local contact and some off-road wheels). The dry climate means little change between seasons, the water (while not exactly warm) is less chilly than further south, and all the empty desert makes for mighty clear skies - apparently some of the clearest in the world - astronomers ahoy!

The capital city of the region, affectionately referred to as 'Antofa' by the locals, is now a hub for copper mining (previously saltpeter and silver) with a mix of mall culture and old-fashioned heritage monuments around Barrio Histórico - the historical center, and some British influences such as the Torre Reloj clock tower - a reproduction of London's Big Ben. To the north of Antofa, Tocopilla and Mejillones might appeal more to non-so-big-city-lovers, poblados (settlements) such as Hornitos and Caleta Buena have quaint fishermen-come-holiday-cabin vibes. The most lasting impressions are undoubtedly from the natural wonders; like the imposing volcanic rock-arch, La Portada, the sweet little Isla Santa María, and the canyons and caves that reveal the long ago stories of these lands.

Driving tip: going south from Antofagasta city, you'll hit an inland stretch of Ruta 5.. maybe if the long drive ahead feels tiring you feel tempted to stay on this road, hop skip a bit of ocean view? We recommend you take the other option: fill up your fuel tank at La Negra (next fuel stop not till Taltal on this route) and take Ruta 1 for the magical seaside ride from El Cobre to Taltal. The road's fairly new and not too traffic-infested, so you've about 150 kms of a beautiful drive - plenty time to keep an eye out for quality peaks in remote spots to mindsurf.

TO DO

◆

See the beauty of the coast on a kayak or canoe paddle to Isla Santa María and/or La Portada with **Nortexpediciones (38)**.

They've professional, experienced guides with lots of knowledge to share about the wildlife in the area - from wolves to sea lions, boobies and the Pingüino de Humboldt - and are eager to share the magical sights. Tours range from 4 hours up to a 2-day adventure and overnight camping, with a variety of offerings from low difficulty to expert, and can include a trek if you want to explore on land too. They also arrange separate trekking and bicycle tours if you're not in the mood to get wet. Open all year.

a. II región, Antofagasta
t. +56 9 9516 3851
w. nortexpediciones.cl

Join the knowledgeable guides of **Ruhiscos Aventuras (39)** to descubre las joyas (discover the jewels) of the region. They've a grand menu of tours and treks which extend to the whole region, from an inland adventure to the volcano and hot springs of Parque Nacional Llullaillaco to a hike through canyons to see the historical cave paintings at Quebrada del Medano, just north of Taltal. Closer to the city, visit the rock arch La Portada, the ruins of Huanchaca, and the Mano del Desierto - a 10-meter-tall sculpture of a hand reaching out from the sands of the Atacama Desert. You'll learn plenty about the history, geography, flora and fauna of the area, and then some.. astronomy's their specialist subject, so there'll also be some stories about the skies above. If astronomy's all you're interested in, check out the night tours such as their Toca las Estrelas (touch the stars) en Chacabuco and El Medano de Atacama (astronomical center) trips. Open all year.

a. Oficina Petronila 271 Casa 33, Antofagasta
t. +56 9 6319 6101
w. ruhiscos.cl

Built in the 1800s, the **Museo de Antofagasta** (40) is housed in a former customs office, constructed in a U-shape and orientated towards the sea. Entry is free and you can easily while away an hour or two learning about the cultural heritage of the region. Open all year.

a. Avenida Balmaceda 2786, Antofagasta
t. +56 55 222 7016
w. museodeantofagasta.gob.cl

Bouldering gym and climbing school **Gecko Boulder** (41) began as the project of 4 friends and grew into a popular facility for all levels. They offer lessons for adults and children, or a day pass at a reasonable price, and have a little shop selling climbing accessories and energy snacks, with a small gym area too. Open all year. ◆$◆

a. Angamo 0393, Antofagasta
t. +56 9 7703 9231
fb. Gecko Boulder Antofagasta

EAT/DRINK/HANG OUT
◆

Find generous portions of traditional local dishes, mainly empanadas and seafood, and a warm atmosphere at **Restaurant La Normita** (42) in the little seaside settlement Caleta Buena. Popular with locals and visitors alike for almost 20 years, you can eat in or get a takeout and wander along to the beach, where a few tables and chairs are set out. Open all year. ◆$$◆

a. Manzana 4, Caleta Buena
t. +56 9 8580 9978
i. restolanormita

Cantina 309 (43) are known for serving refreshing cocktails and exquisite pizzas with a stunning view over the beach of Hornito. Based in the southern section of the playa, they're open for lunch, dinner, and drinks till late. They've a sleep option too (apartments) in case you want to stay over and sample every cocktail on the menu. Open all year. ◆$$◆

a. Avenida Hornito 309, Mejillones
t. +56 9 9887 6664
w. aparthornito.cl

An innovative menu of authentic Peruvian dishes awaits your delight at **Restaurant La Cholita** (44). The joyful décor has a colorful bric-a-brac style in a light and spacious room, service is friendly and the food's fresh and full of flavor. At time of writing, they await their alcohol licence so call and check they have it by now if you anticipate wine with your meal - best to call and book ahead anyway, especially at weekends. Open all year. ◆$$◆

a. Avenida San Martín 846, Mejillones
t. +56 9 6150 1830
fb. lacholitarestaurante

Straight across the main avenue from the seaside promenade, in between the Balneario Municipal and the (small but new and with a seaview) skate park, **La Pulpería Gourmet** (45) is a quiet little coffee haven to get your caffeine fix and some freshly baked pastries, cakes or snacks. Open all year. ◆$◆ ◆$$◆

a. Avenida República de Croacia 086, Antofagasta
t. +56 9 9712 7279
fb. La Pulperia Coffee

A good spot to keep one eye on the surf at Llacolén while enjoying a drink or a bite; the wooden beach hut, **Kiosko Llacolen** (46), serves snacks, sandwiches, drinks and ice cream. Seasonal opening. ◆$◆ ◆$$◆

a. Avenida Jaime Guzman, Antofagasta

Get your snack-attack satisfaction here! Sandwiches loaded with big fillings are available at **La Maestra Sanguchería** (47) and can be snacked upon on their very nice terrace. The menu's stuffed with muy meat-feasts (hamburguesas, hot dogs, steaks etc) but they've also some veggie falafel pankos for the non-carne-eaters. Open all year. ◆$$◆ ◆$$$◆

a. Antonio Toro 1026, Antofagasta
t. +56 9 6606 3511
w. lamaestra.cl

Antofa's fine dining option, **Amares Bistro** (48) offers a taste of coastal-Peruvian fusion. A casual-but-sophisticated place, you'll find the food creative, the wine selection extensive and the pisco sour as snappy as the interior design. We recommend you make a reservation - it's a popular city hotspot with a few awards and a flurry of rave reviews. Open all year. ♦$$$$♦

a. Antonio Toro 995, Antofagasta
t. +56 9 4672 0804
w. amares.cl

SLEEP
♦

Based in Caleta Buena, **Kai Tour Eco Hostel (49)** have a cluster of rustic wooden cabins around a communal outdoor area with small pool, shared kitchen and bathroom facilities. Offering relaxed vibes, old campervan décor and sunset bonfires right by the beach, the accommodation's suitable for all types of travelers, families included, with basic but clean and comfy-looking single, double and bunk rooms. Choose to stay only, or

additional options; from surf, wakeboard and SUP lessons and tours to yoga and massages. Open all year. ♦$$♦

a. Manzana 2, Sitio 8, Caleta Buena
t. +56 9 3405 2137
i. kaitourtocopilla

Nothing fancy but simple wooden cabanas on the main avenue, close to the shopping center and Playa Mejillones and only 30-minutes' drive to Hornitos. **Cabañas Hostal Alojamiento Inhome Mejillones (50)** have parking, are equipped with mini-kitchen and fridge, and have hot water and wifi. What more do you need! Open all year. ♦$$♦

a. Avenida San Martín 643, Mejillones
t. +56 9 9081 5493
w. inhomemejillones.negocio.site

Surf Hostel Antofagasta (51) is a very basic stay but straight across the road from the beach, on the tail end of the city. Open all year. ♦$♦ ♦$$♦

a. Calle Baja 07040, El Huascar, Antofagasta
t. +56 9 8708 4217
i. surfhostelantofagasta

A short walk from Plaza Colón and the city's main attractions, **Hotel Paula (52)** has a business-trip kinda vibe but with a homey feel. A few minutes away from Antofa's best beaches. Open all year. ♦$$$♦

a. Manuel Antonio Matta 2469, Antofagasta
t. +56 55 226 8989
w. hotelpaola.cl

Just north of the village of Taltal, **Cabañas Caleta Hueso (53)** have some nicely done up fully equipped cabanas around a small pool, and an ocean view. Find clever decorative use of some equipment from the days of gold mining in the Trapiche style. Each cabana has a small decking area and on-site bar/restaurant, La Changuita, serves good food and great mojitos. Open all year. ♦$$♦

a. Ruta 1 260,
Kilometro 2 Camino a Paposo, Taltal
t. +56 9 9152 9691
w. caletahueso.cl

City stay with a friendly atmosphere, **Paposo Inn Hostel (54)** has a few shared dorms and facilities, or choose a private room with its own bathroom. A clean and comfortable place with a nice courtyard, well equipped kitchen, hot water and good wifi. Open all year. ♦$$♦

a. Serrano 215, Taltal
t. +56 9 9999 7788

SURF

Norte Grande has countless surf spots, from north of Arica to south of Antofagasta. If you're keen on surfing reefs, here's your go-to. You'll find surf shops, surf schools, and lively hubs along the most popular breaks. Surf here is as consistent as an eat, sleep, surf, repeat cycle, even in summer, and corduroy lines from shore to horizon will gratify your wave-seeking soul more often than not.

ARICA (I)

You can expect the surf area nearest Peru's border to be dry and sunny, but never too hot in summer, never too cold in winter. The water temperature's slightly warmer than the rest of Chile. Only slightly! The first report of surfers here was in the 1970s; intrepid Peruvians and Chileans, together with a handful of visitors from other continents, exploring beyond borders up to the gnarliest of slabs at the very tip of the Alacrán peninsula, like the famous **El Gringo**. There are several spots offering fast, hollow waves - mostly reefs - along the peninsula; all needing medium to big swells to work and an advanced to expert level. Seek local knowledge. And be sure you've the experience and skills to handle it before you jump in.

Not up to slabby barrels? We recommend these consistent beach breaks:

In 1983, one of the first surf championships in Chile was held at **Las Machas**. The endless beach, a little north of Arica, is suitable for all levels (depending on conditions) and works best with small to medium SW swells towards high tide. Crowds spread out over several peaks but it can get busy. ◆ *All levels/sand/easy parking.* ◆

Breaking near town, find **El Tubo** and **Playa Chinchorro**. Playa Chinchorro is a popular family beach and therefore more crowded than other beaches in the area. With peaks to choose from, this beach break works best on smaller SW swells with not too much wind, as will El Tubo. The latter's less powerful than its name implies. Higher tides are preferable for both spots and you'll find a lively buzz around from restaurants and surf schools. ◆ *All levels/sand/shower/toilet/restaurant/ surf shop/surf school/easy parking.* ◆

Black sand beach **Arenillas Negras** is less consistent than the above and exposed, so it picks up wind easily - works for kite surfers though. Best at mid tide in small to medium SW and W swells. Beware of rips and rocks. ◆ *All levels/sand and rocks/easy parking.* ◆

to handle fast tubes over shallow reef. With Iquique's main road running along the coast, in parts you can surf-check easily as you drive along it. The waves break mostly on reef and rock bottom - a spectacle to watch when big. All along this section of powerful waves and advanced level spots, such as **Colegio** and **Punta Una**, you'll find surf shops and restaurants. There are a few beach breaks to be found too if you're unsure about surfing reefs (or didn't bring your booties!). Most beach breaks work best on small swells, usually in the morning - before the wind gets strong and messes up the waves.

El Faro, at the city's popular Playa Cavancha, can be enjoyed by every level of surfer. Works best with small to medium SW, W and NW swells, from low to mid tide. ◆ *All levels/shower/ toilet/restaurant/surf shop/surf school/ easy parking except in summer.* ◆

level, and again, best to seek local knowledge for entrance points and hazards. South of town, the reef break La Cúpula (or **Playa Llacoleen**) is a national contest site - considered one of the best waves in the area, it can get crowded with skillful surfers on good days. Works best on medium SW swells, beware of rocks and urchins.

Seaside resort **Hornitos**, some 80 km north of Antofagasta, attracts Antofagasta beachgoers and surfers alike. The beautiful beach is surrounded by sand cliffs and colorful off-grid holiday homes. The vibe tends to be eco-friendly, and visitors usually hold to the leave no trace etiquette, with utmost respect to the environment. Works best with a small W swell on clean windless days. ◆ *All levels/sand/ easy parking.* ◆

IQUIQUE (II)
◆

With 400 km between them, you can only imagine how many waves and spots from Arica to the next surf hub, Iquique, remain unridden, untouched or undiscovered. You'll want a solid ride to explore, and probably need to be an expert rider as well - both car and board wise. If you do see someone out there, chances are it's a skilled bodyboarder who knows how

ANTOFAGASTA (III)
◆

Another 400 kms south of Iquique you'll reach Antofagasta, with the same unexplored, wild options between the two surf hubs. If you do explore, tread carefully and wisely. Just saying. Around Antofagasta are some reef breaks that need big swells to work. **Piedra del Lobo**, **La Puntilla** and **La Portada** work on medium swells too. All are advanced

CHILE

SCHOOL RENTAL SHOP

ARICA

Surf Olas Chile (**55**) is located at the south end of Playa Las Machas, near town. The right place if you want to rent equipment, join a surf lesson or just like to hang out and grab some healthy snacks at their shaded beach cabana. Open all year.

a. Avenida Eilat, Playa Las Machas, Arica
t. +56 9 7616 4588

Find **Escuela de Surf Akua** (**56**) at Akua Natural Café. Surf lessons and rentals on offer, as well as perfectly

tasty pre and post surf coffees and food. Open all year.

a. Ingeniero Raúl Pey Casado 3300, Arica
t. +56 9 5324 6694
i. escueladesurfakua

Another surf school also serving as a friendly beachside coffee shop is

Punto Surf Arica (**57**). Open all year, low season opening times vary.

a. Ingeniero Raúl Pey Casado 3336, Arica
t. +56 9 8271 5170
i. aricapuntosurf

IQUIQUE

Vertical Surf Shop (**58**) has about all and everything you might need surfing-wise, and is conveniently located opposite the beach and surf spot El Colegio. Find wax, leashes, the works, and knowledgeable owner Sergio. Surf school **Punto Norte** (**59**), at the same address, offers lessons and rentals. Open all year.

a. Arturo Prat 580, Iquique
t. +56 9 9886 8631 (shop) /
   9 9414 3563 (school)
i. punto_norte_surf

Find surf school **UmaJaqi** (**60**) at Playa Cavancha, run by welcoming local family Hernandez. Besides lessons they also organize surf safaris. Seasonal opening times vary.

a. Playa Cavancha, Iquique
t. +56 9 6727 9145
w. umajaqi.cl

Like their neighbors (UmaJaqi), surf school **Ecorider** (**61**) have their space right at the beach of Cavancha. Surf and bodyboard lessons for all levels and ages. Open all year.

a. Playa Cavancha, Iquique
t. +56 9 6819 8849
fb. Escuela de Surf Ecoriders

With the owner Victor Lopez Lagos dedicated to teaching all things surf and ocean, he founded **Escuela de Surf y Bodyboard Arturo Prat** (**62**). Private or group surf, SUP and bodyboard lessons on offer for all levels. Open all year.

a. Playa Cavancha, Iquique
t. +56 9 5927 1982
w. surfbodyboardarturoprat.cl

ANTOFAGASTA

In the south of town, opposite Playa Blanca, find **Padang Surf Shop** (**63**). They've all surf necessities, friendly staff, and offer surf lessons and rental of equipment too. Open all year.

a. Avenida República de Croacia 105, Antofagasta
t. +56 55 320 9153
i. padangsurfshopantofagasta

SEASIDE LOCAL: LORENA FICA

Born and raised in the seaside resort Arica, well known for its famous El Gringo break, Lorena Fica grew up in a family of ocean lovers. From the moment she first paddled out, at the age of 11 years, it was clear that surfing would become her portal to achieve grand things in life.

With a fire and determination that characterize her, Lorena faced many hurdles to become the first professional Chilean female surfer. The biggest hurdle being the competitions; at the time she started surfing there wasn't a junior division for girls in Chile. So, she joined the boys. By the time there were divisions for women, things hadn't improved much - there were very few women surfing at high level, so often there was only one round.

"Becoming a professional surfer wasn't really a decision, it was more a gift, a sport that I loved deeply. I was born with a lot of perseverance. That, and tons of discipline, I think, led me to having a professional career in this sport."

Today, with over 16 years of her sports career and many national and international wins under her belt, she's (almost singlehandedly) narrowed the local gap between men and women in surfing. Lorena's been listed as one of The Pioneering Women of Chile, The 100 Young Leaders, The 100 Leading Women and, on top of that, was one of the highest ranking Chileans in the World Surf League in 2019.

Besides all her achievements as an athlete, wins and losses in competitions, Lorena also grew as a person. She learned at some point that no matter what you do, but especially when competing, it's important not to overlook the fun of it all, and equally so to stay open-minded.

"When you´re trying to be competitive, many times during our long career in this sport we forget about enjoying it. And it has happened to me before and I think that´s the worst thing we can do to ourselves. I think that surfing is done to enjoy, it is a sport that requires a lot of connection, gives all sorts of sensations, and the fact of forgetting that, forgetting to have a good time in the sea, I think it harms us a lot."

FAMILY AND THE OCEAN

While in her late twenties, along with competing she fulfilled another childhood dream; of having a seaside hostel. The Phuqata Surf Camp in Arica, which Lorena runs with her family, is a place where travelers can connect with the local community.

"Since I was 15 years old, I said that one day I wanted to have my own hostel. Because of surfing you travel much and stay in lots of hostels and have different experiences. I wanted to share that. Running a hostel really caught my attention, and I felt that it was the type of entrepreneurship I wanted to do, a thing that brings value to the community."

As for spending most of her time by or in the ocean, it's an obvious choice…

"For me the sea is everything, the opportunity to change a bad day in an instant by just touching the water. I think the connection I have with the sea is something very special. My upbringing was closely linked to the sea, so it's about having beautiful memories. I think that for me it is always like a part of my family, or something that will always keep me close to my family and is linked to my family, since they are also lovers of the ocean."

A STRONG MIND

♦

When faced with fears or the challenge of overcoming difficulties, Lorena tries humor, and knows the key to success is having a strong mind.

"Many times, I have had this feeling of fear - especially in big waves or in waves with rocks or reefs where I know that I can hit really hard, or that the wave can keep me underwater for a long time. At that moment I know that I have to be calm. So, before doing it I prepare myself and one of my mantras to face this is…(giggles) 'I prefer to die than not surf!'"

"I think that every lifestyle, even more so when one has ambitious goals, there is always the cost of achieving those goals. In my case, I think that the most difficult thing to face is being away from my family for many months, traveling the world. It is very stressful to be constantly competing and, in general, you lose more than you win, so the frustrations are huge. However, obviously I feel that I have a privileged life in that sense, and I've had to work hard on my mindset, to have a very strong mind and to not care what people say."

ON TRAVELING

♦

With competitions worldwide, from the USA to Australia, Europe, Africa and countries nearby, traveling's been on the menu for Lorena from an early age. Despite missing her home and family, roaming the globe enriched her life.

"Some of the best moments in my life, living this lifestyle, are the experiences I share with people, what surfing gives you. As the cliché goes, friends are the family one chooses, and I think that surfing has given me that family. I've been able to mature a lot spending time with people who've had different experiences, or maybe have lived through very hard things, strong people that I might never have encountered in my life otherwise."

"What I like most about traveling is that it never becomes a routine, there is always something different: different waves, getting out of your comfort zone. I think that is what I like the most, you grow while traveling, meeting different people, seeing places - I think that's amazing."

But of all the places she's seen and been, home is where her heart is.

"Obviously one of my favorite places in Chile is Arica, I really find it incredible. More so if you are a surfer. Then there are several places and waves that I like, for example Puertecillo, Pullay, the atmosphere of Pichilemu… I have great friends there. Also the central zone, really, there are so many different and incredibly magical places. The whole Ñuble region is a super magical place too."

And while she's not traveling, where will we most likely run into Lorena?

"While I am in Arica, everyone knows that in the mornings they find me in the proximity of El Pipo beach, La Playa las Machas. That's my place for sure."

♦

Want to follow Lorena's surfing and life adventures, or maybe want to spend some time at Phuqata Surf Hostel? **i.** @lorenafica / @phuqata_surfhostel / **w.** phuqatahostel.com

♦

BALANCING: VRKSASANA

◆

Tree Pose

Standing on one leg helps prepare you to find balance - on the board or in any movement that requires it. This pose also enhances your focus while balancing.

The practice of yoga brings many benefits, especially for surfing; building your strength and flexibility. It also helps you find a higher level of concentration, as well as ease, by using what's called 'Drishti' in Sanskrit - a soft but concentrated gaze that helps you stay present in the moment.

Benefits:
Strengthens the legs, ankle muscles and core, opens up the hips. On a more subtle level, it activates your nervous system, aids coordination and builds stamina.

How:
Stand with your feet shoulder-width apart. Focus on a point in front of you to help you find balance (yep, that's Drishti). Shift your weight onto your right foot. Lift your left knee and bring it out to the side. Depending on your range of motion and how steady you feel, place your left foot on either your right ankle, calf, or inner thigh (while pushing with your thigh against your foot too). Hold as long as you feel comfortable, while breathing calmly. Then shake it out (if that feels good) and repeat on the other side.

IN AND AROUND PORTOFINO TO BAHIA INGLESA

♦

If you're coming from the north, you've spent some time already in the clear-sky Atacama Desert - the 1000 km-long band of white sand considered the driest desert in the world, rich in mineral resources, referred to as the landscape closest resembling Mars. But now you enter the Atacama region, you've a chance to see the much-acclaimed Desert Bloom - 'Desierto Florido'. If spring brings unusually high (El Niño style) rainfall, the latent seeds and bulbs of over 200 species of flowering plants create this phenomenal multicolor carpet. The bloom spreads across the coastal range from Copiapó to Vallenar from September through November. Worthy of route planning to be here and hope to see, and if you do… get all the photos you can but be mindful that the precious bloom's protected and anyone who damages it will be fined. If you're not lucky enough to see it in all its splendor, you should be happy enough with the cacti, tuco-tuco (chinchilla-like rodents), four-eyed frogs, foxes and guanacos (ancestor of the llama) to look out for. And the beautiful sunny beaches, of course.

From Chañaral in the north, down past the capital city, Copiapó, to the small port city Huasco, find a mixture of city beaches and solitary remote spots along the coastline. With sweet humble surfy towns like Portofino Atacama and its magnificent righthander, city life around Caldera and Copiapó, and virgin-sand clear-water spots like Puerto Viejo's Playa La Virgen, you've plenty of seaside-vibe options to choose from, and valleys booming with fruit in between. Once big for silver mining; iron, copper and gold have also brought wealth to the Atacama region, where the fertile Huasco Valley, known as the Garden of Atacama, is well known for its pisco-producing vines.

The small seaside resort town of Bahía Inglesa, apparently named after British pirates who took refuge here back in the 17th century, has a more modern and much less brown appearance than the generally dry and dusty landscape of Chile's desert regions. Stories abound of buccaneers' buried treasure all along this coast, as well as pirate ships wrecked not far off the coast. Not too built up, despite its popularity, Bahía Inglesa is best known for its beaches with Caribbean-like colors. But don't let that fool you into thinking the water's as warm.

TO DO

◆

The coastal natural reserve **Pan de Azúcar National Park** (**1**) offers magical trails to Pan de Azúcar Island, the Las Chatas islets, the emerging Las Mariposas (butterfly) rocks, and the beaches Blanca, Piqueros and El Soldado. Look out for the Humboldt penguin, guanacos and Yunco Ducks. Staffed by a CONAF park ranger who can advise you about trails and what to look out for where, boat rides around Pan de Azúcar Island are available, there are designated camping areas and cabañas (see Sleep section), and restaurants within the park. There's a small entrance fee, open all year.

a. Pan de Azúcar National Park, Chañaral
t. +56 52 221 3404
w. conaf.cl/parques/parque-nacional-pan-de-azucar

Curious about rocks (or into bouldering)? We can highly recommend the Zoológico Piedra, known as the **Stone Zoo** (**2**). About halfway between Portofino and Bahía Inglesa on the Panamericana Norte, zoomorphic rocks sculpted by erosion over thousands of years are within a signposted circuit. The circuit can be done by vehicle or on foot and is an ideal place for bouldering. Bring a bag to take your trash away with you (and get karma bonus points if you take some that was left behind by someone less considerate than you). Open all year.

a. Ruta 5, Km 12, Caldera
fb. Zoológico de Piedras Atacama

Find the block-wide **skatepark in Caldera** (**3**) located next to the south side of the stadium, Estadio La Caldera. Full of bowls, stairs, handrails and more. Open all year.

a. Avenida Canal Beagle, Caldera

The team at **Chango Adventure** (**4**) are group of young professionals who love the sea, nature and watersports. In 2015 they came together to revive the ancient routes of the ancient Camanchaco or Chango people and discover the marine biodiversity of the Atacama region. And they're keen to share it with us! Between them they tick all the boxes as surfers, lifeguards, climbers, photographers, first aiders, tour guides and kayak instructors, so you should be in safe hands to go for a paddle (kayak or SUP) with them and discover the coastal delights.

They can also take you climbing and/or organize a paddle-climb combo. Open all year.

a. Isla Lenox 533, Caldera
t. +56 9 8723 8442
w. changoadventure.com

In 2010, 33 Chilean miners were trapped 700 meters underground in the copper-gold mine **Mina San José** (**5**). After 69 days, the miners were successfully rescued - to date this is the largest and most successful rescue operation in the history of mining worldwide. The mine was closed after the accident and is now run by the government as a tourist attraction (with a viewpoint and info boards; you can't go down into the mine, obvs) to pay homage to the miners and the happy ending. About half an hour drive east from Caldera/Bahía Inglesa, free access, open all year.

a. Mina San José, C-351 Copiapó

The talented hands of Pamela in Bahía Inglesa have treated many a renowned celeb, including (so it's said) none other than Antonio Banderas. Find her in a small wooden shack surrounded by plants, overlooking the beach in front of Hotel Rocas de Bahía if you want to treat yourself to a **Quartz Bed Massage** (**6**). If she's busy with another client when you arrive, you can relax on the quartz beds while you wait. Seasonal opening.

a. Avenida El Morro 1, Bahía Inglesa
t. +56 9 8383 5809

The invitation from the clear turquoise waters of Bahía Inglesa to explore is hard to resist. **Bahía Mako Diving Center** (**7**) offers equipment hire, introductions and courses for beginners and guided expeditions for experienced divers. They also organize snorkeling trips. Located on the main avenue next to the beach. Open all year.

a. Avenida El Morro 610, Bahía Inglesa
t. +56 9 4631 9177
fb. Bahía Mako

40 kilometers north of the picturesque fishing port Huasco, **Coastal Desert National Park Llanos de Challe** (**8**) is even quieter and more remote than its surroundings, which are pretty quiet and remote most of the time. Unless the desert bloom's flowering. The most popular hike is the 2.5 km self-guided Centennial Interpretive Trail, a circular route from the Los Pozos Sector Nursery. Or go large on the 6 km Los Corrales Trail. There's an Environmental Information Center, park rangers providing a welcome talk, picnic areas, camping available overlooking Playa Blanca (and a food truck that drives through the park each morning selling essentials like fresh bread, eggs and veggies). Wanna stay forever? Well, it's open all year, so you kinda could.

a. Parque Nacional Llanos del Challe
t. +56 51 261 1555
w. conaf.cl/parques/parque-nacional-llanos-de-challe

From the 22-meter high **Faro Monumental de Huasco** (**9**) you've a lovely view over the picturesque fishing port and beaches as well as a fine vista over the hills around. If that's not exciting enough for you and you need a little adrenaline pump, check out the **skatepark** (**10**) just a

15-minute walk east along Ignacio Carrera Pinto. Open all year.

a. Punta Escorial, Huasco

Follow Río Huasco along the valley east to Vallenar to get some pisco from the source at the **Jahir Saba Distillery (11)**, **Destileria Nacional SpA**. While there, you can learn some about what makes the Chilean pisco so different to the Peruvian version, enjoy a view over the city, grab a coffee, or go to town and drink or dine in the exquisite bar-restaurant Museo del Pisco. The drive itself can be a bit of a gobsmacker; the fruit-filled green valley feeling particularly surreal if you've done endless days of desert, rocks and cacti. (Tip: If you get a taste for pisco tasting, you can follow the pisco trail inland, passing some pretty picturesque towns to Alto del Carmen, then on to San Félix to try the piscos of Bou Barroeta and Horcón Quemado, or branch off to El Tránsito to the distillery of Armadita.

Tip 2: You might want to designate a driver who isn't so enthusiastic about the sampling - it's a fair drive!) Open all year from lunchtime till midnight.

a. Calle Chungara 1427, Vallenar
t. +56 9 4282 2659
w. piscosaba.cl

EAT/DRINK/HANG OUT

◆

Pet-friendly beach terrace snack bar **Roots (12)** has good vibes and funky music, and serves proper coffees, acai bowls and tasty sandwiches, along with a selection of seriously tempting freshly baked cakes and bakes (vegan options too). Open all year. ◆$$◆ ◆$$$◆

a. Avenida El Morro, Bahía Inglesa
i. roots_bahiainglesa

Peruvian food and local seafood are on offer at **Domo Lounge (13)** restobar, situated in a terrace with a dome above it, overlooking the beach. Open till late, with regular live music and a good cocktail menu. Open all year. ◆$$$◆

a. Avenida El Morro 610, Bahía Inglesa
t. +56 9 6244 6823
i. domolounge

Coral Restaurant (14) at the hotel Coral De Bahía is a cool (parasols and palm trees provide shade on the ocean-view terrace) stop for a good meal. Offering a Chilean-Fusion-seafood menu, the Coral was the first restaurant in Bahía Inglesa, opened 35 years ago by a (now retired) well-known local diver and chef. Open all year. ◆$$$◆

a. Avenida El Morro 564, Bahía Inglesa
t. +56 52 231 9160
w. coraldebahia.cl

Ostiones Vivos (15). As per the name - live oysters, served just about as fresh as you can get on the pier, with salt, lemon and merquén. Seasonal opening. ◆$$◆

a. Calle Copiapó, Bahía Inglesa

For a quick bite, like an empanada or pizza, drop into **Naturalia (16)**. The small place, close to the beach, offers friendly efficient service so you can refuel fast and get back in the water pronto. Open all year. ◆$◆ ◆$$◆

a. Calle Miramar 182, Bahía Inglesa
t. +56 9 8758 4481
fb. NaturaliaBahia

Best make a reservation if you'd like to lunch at popular seafood restaurant **Tumorrou (17)** and be sure to bring some cash with you. Or get there early and be prepared to queue. Located approximately 10 minutes' drive south from Bahía Inglesa, overlooking Playa El Morro, you'll find a rustic beach bar set-up, chilled atmosphere, great view, good food and some veggie options on the menu too. Open all year.
◆$$◆ ◆$$$◆

a. Km 8 al sur de Bahía Inglesa
t. +56 9 9627 7965
fb. Tumorrou Bahía Inglesa

SHOP
◆

The cute tiny wooden shop by the beach, **Inti Bahía (18)** sells regional products; clothing, crafts, wooden toys and suchlike. If you're after a souvenir or keepsake, it's worth a pop-in and see. It also serves as the local tourism agency point. Seasonal opening.

a. Bahía Inglesa
t. +56 9 3175 1840
i. inti_bahia

SLEEP
◆

Find peaceful ecological camping grounds with magical views, domos and cabins (sleeping up to 8) within the Parque Nacional at **Pan De Azucar Lodge (19)**. There are two areas to choose from, one at Playa Piqueros the other at El Soldado. There's an outdoor spa, activities like trekking and yoga and some workshops. Open all year. ◆$$◆

a. Parque Nacional Pan de Azucar, Ruta C 120, Chañaral
t. +56 9 9844 7375
w. pandeazucarlodge.cl

Beach campsite **Los Yecos (20)** in Playa Los Piqueros is another basic stay with a 5-star view option within the Pan de Azucar National Park. You can park your van or pitch a tent and enjoy the not-a-lot-but-nature surroundings, including foxes and guanacos that come mooching curiously around. They also organize outdoor exploring activities like trekking, diving and snorkeling. Seasonal opening.
◆$◆ ◆$$◆

a. Parque Nacional Pan de Azucar, Ruta C 120, Chañaral
t. +56 9 9230 8728
i. campinglosyecos

Brothers Rodolfo and Nicolas, surfers themselves, came to Portofino one fine day with some construction material (still in progress) and claimed a piece of desert land meters away from the very consistent surf break of Portofino to build their dream; **Portofino Surf Camp (21)**. They also built a skatebowl in the middle of the site, so you can practice your moves in between surf sessions. Open all year.
◆$$◆

a. Ruta C-260, Portofino
t. +56 9 8267 0901
i. portofinosurfcamp

You can't miss **Hotel Rocas de Bahía** (**22**) with its colorful pink facade, never mind that it's probably the biggest hotel in Bahía Inglesa. Right next to the beach, bars and restaurants, the rooms have a great ocean view, as do the bar and restaurant on the top floor. They've a swimming pool outside and if you're wearing your guayabera shirt you'll fit right in, and feel like you're on the set of a 90s movie. The atmosphere's definitely most hip and happening during summer. Open all year. ◆$$$◆ ◆$$$$◆

a. Avenida El Morro 88, Bahía Inglesa
t. +56 52 231 6005
w. rocasdebahia.cl

80 meters away from the main beach, all's white at **Hotel Blanco Encalada** (**23**). Named after a naval ship that went down off the Caldera coast in 1891 during the civil war (historical factoid: the first ship in the world to be sunk after being hit by a self-propelled torpedo), the building's also designed in naval ship style with porthole windows and some interesting angles. Inside, find clean and comfortable single, double, triple and quadruple rooms and staff who want to provide the best service to ensure you a wonderful experience. Open all year. ◆$$$◆

a. Copiapó 514, Bahía Inglesa
t. +56 9 9886 8337
w. hotelblancoencalada.cl

Based right on the beach, **Domo Camping** (**24**) have domes that are on raised wooden platforms, each with a small terrace, and have a panoramic view over Morro La Ballena, Playa Las Machas and the Atacama Desert. Shared (very basic) shower and toilet

facilities and breakfast included. Open all year. ◆$◆ ◆$$◆

a. Avenida El Cisne Km 1.8, Playa Las Machas, Bahía Inglesa
t. +56 9 7648 3784
w. domocamping.cl

The slightly more upmarket and family-friendly camping option just 600m from the beach, **Bahia Club** (**25**) sites include a canopied area with picnic table and electricity, shared swimming pool and jacuzzi, communal

bathrooms and laundry room. Pets are welcome. Cabanas are available too - fully furnished and equipped. Open all year. ◆$◆ ◆$$◆

a. Vía 1-A, Playa Las Machas, Bahía Inglesa
t. +56 9 8429 9950
w. bahiaclub.com

The comfortable and nicely decorated cabanas for up to 5 people of **Cabanas Ecologicas (26)** are just 500 meters from Playa Rocas Negras, with fully equipped kitchens. Guests have free use of bicycles during their stay to go and explore. Open all year.
◆$$◆ ◆$$$◆

a. Ruta 302, Rocas Negras, Bahía Inglesa
t. +56 9 8380 1503
w. cabanasecologicas.cl

Paradisical beach **Playa la Virgen (27)** is top of the hotspots for lush lazing on the beach time around these parts. In the middle of nowhere with nothing going on - the nearest town, Puerto Viejo has not a lot going on either, besides beach life. Camping options here are surprisingly tidy and organized, with each pitch (vans/tents) having a small canopied picnic/grill area, lighting and a USB port (mod-cons in abundance!) and private bathroom. Cabanas and casas in Robinson Crusoe style, ranging in size from mini to quite massive, are available too. The owners are conscious of the environment and careful with water, energy and waste, as well as caring about the native flora and fauna - tidy considerate guests are very welcome. Open all year.
◆$$◆ ◆$$$◆

a. Playa La Virgen, Puerto Viejo
t. +56 52 235 8050
w. playalavirgen.cl

On the outskirts of the small city of Huasco, **Atacama Glamp (28)** is nicely located between the skatepark and Playa Grande with a view over the wetlands. Rock up in your van and camp, pitch your own tent or rent a fully equipped yurt and glamp. They've a communal area for cooking and socializing, clean bathrooms with hot showers, and bikes and kayaks for guests to use. The friendly helpful owners are happy to give advice on the area and regularly organize yoga/kitesurf/surf activities and classes as well as eco workshops. Open all year.
◆$◆

a. Ignacio Carrera Pinto, Huasco
t. +56 9 6413 8430
i. atacamaglamp

IN AND AROUND LA SERENA AND TOTORALILLO

•

The beauties of the Coquimbo region are not only on the surface but also underwater, and (especially) in the skies. From Punta de Choros through La Serena - the capital of the region, second oldest city in Chile - down to Pichidangui, a fine mix of desert, lush valleys, mountain ranges and long sandy beaches with beautiful clear waters provide a playground terrain for every kind of explorer. The Andes mountains are closest to the ocean here in the country's narrowest region, and while some of the towns (especially in the dusty north) are less colorful, if all you need's a place to sleep so you can reach the ocean, you'll find they serve just fine as portals to the waterworld.

The Reserva Nacional Pinguino de Humboldt's the main attraction of the north, with a smorgasbord of marine life to be seen; from whales to dolphins, otters and sea lions, fur seals and seabirds aplenty - very likely some of the famous penguins the conservation area's named after. Inland to the east of La Serena, the Elqui Valley is a name well-known by fans of wine, pisco and astronomy. Find the Limarí Valley a couple of hours south if you crave a bit more wine and pisco sampling. And if you get a taste for being amidst the color green, keep driving south to the Fray Jorge National Park for some jungle time - a refreshing oasis break from dry desert.

The city of La Serena itself is a charming one, with strict building regulations which maintain the neoclassical style architecture. Founded in the 16th century as an important sea link for trade between Santiago and Peru, the 17th century brought pirate raids to its coast and that of its neighbor, the port city of Coquimbo - the City of Churches - which is only a 5km walk from the lighthouse along the waterfront. Aside from boasting many spires, Coquimbo has a sprinkle of colorful buildings and urban art, and can be fun for a few drinks - find Bohemain nightlife, street cafés, pubs and restaurants in the English Quarter, Barrio Inglés.

A popular destination for tourists, stop-off for pilgrims, hub for clusters of astronomers and home to a growing surf community, it can get pretty crowded around the cities in summer. The rest of the year, you'll find a laidback vibe with plenty surf options, from city breaks to barely-a-sign-of-civilization spots like our (outside of summer) favorite, Totoralillo. Tip: If Totoralillo's too crowded for you, you won't have to drive far to find a less people-spattered stretch of sand.

TO DO

◆

Slightly over the border north of the Coquimbo region, Luis Gonzalez and the well qualified crew at **Turismo Orca** (**29**) invite you to join a sustainable adventure to see the magical marine environment of Isla Chañaral - part of the Humboldt Penguins National Reserve. They offer well organized boat tours and scuba diving trips, and have some cabañas too if you want to stop more than a day. Open all year.

a. Las Lapas, Caleta Chañaral de Aceituna
t. +56 9 9640 4844
w. turismosorca.cl

The **Reserva Nacional Pinguino de Humboldt** (**30**) covers the valuable marine ecosystem area around Isla Choros, Isla Damas and Isla Chañaral. Boat tours leave regularly from Punta de Choros (some include landing on Isla Damas to explore a while, depending on time of year and any conservation restrictions in place). It's usually better to go early in the morning or prebook, and make sure to be in a no-hurries-no-worries mood - nobody's in a rush around here. Open all year.

a. Caleta Punta de Choros
t. +56 51 224 4769 (CONAF Coquimbo) / 9 9451 9487 (Turismo Punta de Choros)
w. conaf.cl/parques/reserva-nacional-pinguino-de-humboldt / turismopuntadechoros.cl

Take a trip into Chile's prehistoric past at the **Museo Arqueológico de La Serena** (**31**) and learn the story of the region's people, from the first natives - the Diaguita-Inka - to the arrival of the Europeans. Along with a collection of fascinating artifacts, they've also a monolithic Easter Island stone statue (Moai) carved by the Rapa Nui people. Open all year.

a. Gregorio Cordovéz Esquina Cienfuegos, La Serena
t. +56 51 256 2566
w. museoarqueologicolaserena.gob.cl

About 40 minutes' drive east from La Serena, the 83-meter high Puclaro Dam was built on Río Elqui to form a reservoir, serving the valley with irrigation water. No engine-powered watercraft are allowed in the manmade lake but with reliable wind (pretty much guaranteed from September to April) it makes a mighty fine kite spot. Contact Max, who speaks good English, at **Kitesurf Gualliguaica (32)** to book some lessons, or for info about rental equipment if you're a kite aficionado/a and didn't bring your gear along. He can also advise re windsurf options in the area. Seasonal opening.

- **a.** Kite Center de Puclaro, Gualliguaica, Católica del Norte 212, Vicuña
- **t.** +56 9 3103 2616
- **i.** kitesurf_gualliguaica

If you're into literary greats, meander on up the Elqui Valley to the historic town of Vicuña to visit the birthplace and museum of Chilean Poet Gabriela Mistral, who was awarded the Nobel Prize in 1945. Nearly all info at the **Museo Gabriela Mistral de Vicuña (33)** is in Spanish - a good chance to practice, or simply soak up what you can and enjoy the surrounding landscaped gardens, which all celebrate her life and work. Open from September to May.

- **a.** Gabriela Mistral 759, Vicuña
- **t.** +56 51 266 2262
- **w.** mgmistral.gob.cl

Not buzzing about the poetry corner? The Elqui Valley has plenty other charms to enchant you, including a number of pisco distilleries and vineyards, one of which is **Piuquenes Elqui Vinos y Lodge (34)**, in the

mountains above Vicuña. Meet local wine producers, Juan Luis and Helia and their beloved animals at their family-run magical place to learn the story of their Piuquenes project and products, feel the absolute amor they have for the whole process, and taste their selection of wines, of course! They've poured as much love into their stunning lodge as they do their wines, so check out their accommodation if you fancy a mountain stay... then you've no worries about driving back after a few wines! Open all year.

- **a.** Horcón, S/N, Comuna de Paihuano, Valle de Elqui
- **t.** +56 9 5675 2030
- **w.** piuqueneselqui.cl

Being so bright starry skies in these parts, you'll note **astronomy observatories (35)** popping up all over like teletubby bunkers but errr.. with glass rather than grass roof. There are so many to choose from in the valleys of Elqui, Limarí and Choapa that it's hard to recommend one as top of the popular astronomer spots... so, choose one closest to the location you plan to visit already, close your eyes and point a finger at the map? Or trust a specialist astro-tour guide like Turismo Migrantes, who offer all sorts

of choices (in Spanish or English language) for stargazing and can organize transport, entry, tour, equipment, dinner and sleep options. Their office is based in Pisco Elqui but tours can start from other locations, they've also a menu of other tours (bike, trek, vineyards et al) and are open all year. If you want to go and explore yourself, perhaps check out the Centro Astronomico Alfa Aldea, on the outskirts of Vicuña, or Mamalluca Observatory, 15 minutes' drive north from Vicuña.

- **a.** Coquimbo Region
- **t.** +56 9 6667 3907
- **w.** turismomigrantes.com

Pamper your fine self with a treatment at **Masajes Thalassa Bienestar & Spa (36)** and relieve, relax, rejuvenate, therapy your body into prime condition for the waves. The space Lissette has created is a treat in itself, and she offers aromatherapy and yoga classes too. Open all year.

- **a.** Totoralillo
- **t.** +56 9 6153 0265
- **w.** thalassaterapiasbienestarspa.negocio.site

The UNESCO biosphere reserve, **Parque Nacional Bosque Fray Jorge (37)** is the most northerly rainforest in Chile - a relic of forests that would have covered the land during the last Ice Age, which has survived the arid climate of the Atacama Desert thanks entirely to the camanchaca (coastal fog). Bordered by the

Limarí River to the south and the sea to the west, the park has an education center and some easy trails suitable for any level of walker, some accessible with a wheelchair. Tracks may be slippery though, so mind any sprinting children. All sorts of birdlife can be seen, eagles and hummingbirds among others. Open all year, reduced times during low season. Entrance tickets can be purchased online.

a. Quebrada Varillar, Ovalle
t. +56 51 224 4769
w. conaf.cl/parques/parque-nacional-bosque-fray-jorge

EAT/DRINK/HANG OUT

◆

Abundant portions of curries, noodles and other delicious Asian dishes are on offer at **Lemongrass (38)**. Located in a quiet residential area, they've plenty veggie options and a daily dish of the day on the menu that will save you a few pesos. Open all year. ◆$$◆ ◆$$$◆

a. Las Rojas Ponientes 261, La Serena
t. +56 9 6652 9105
fb. Lemongrass Restaurant La Serena

Homemade burgers and chunky sandwiches served with local artisanal beer from the region, what a combo! The sandwiches at **Ciudad Capital Sandwichería (39)** are some kinda serious, and you can chow down inside or on the terrace (beside the chimenea fire in winter). It's a bit of a walk into the city but that's a fine way to build an apetito! Open all year.
◆$$◆ ◆$$$◆

a. Avenida Gabriel Gonzales Videla 1983, La Serena
t. +56 9 3380 1116
w. ciudadcapitallaserena.cl

Cafeteria Poisson (40) has a relaxed beach bar vibe and serves great coffee and natural juices, with an ocean view to keep an eye on the surf while you tuck into lunch - pizzas, burgers, salads, sandwiches and fresh pastries and bakes. They're vegetarian friendly, and pet friendly too. Open all year. ◆$$◆ ◆$$$◆

a. Avenida del Mar 1001, La Serena
t. +56 9 9573 0119
i. cafeteriapoisson

La Mia Pizza (41) also serves pastas and seafood on their nice terrace overlooking the beach. Open for lunch and dinner, all year. ◆$$◆ ◆$$$◆

a. Avenida del Mar 2100, La Serena
t. +56 51 221 2891
i. lamiapizza.laserena

Get healthy Hawaiian-inspired fast food, poké bowls, kombucha, smoothies and the like at beachside

Kalea Poké (42), where they strive to be plastic-free - just as it should be! Open all year. ◆$◆ ◆$$◆

a. Avenida del Mar 2200, La Serena
t. +56 9 3330 4276
w. kaleapoke.cl

Specialty coffee shop **Lighthouse Coffee (43)** import coffee beans from all over to give you the roast you're after in their cozy place in front of the ocean. Open all year. ◆$$◆ ◆$$$◆

a. Avenida del Mar 2498, La Serena
t. +56 9 2068 4812
i. lighthousecoffeeshop

If you feel like going Greek on the beach, find authentic Mediterranean dishes that'll make you drool (pastas, meat, fish, seafood) and cocktails at **Santorini (44)**. Open all year. ◆$$◆ ◆$$$◆

a. Avenia del Mar 2700, La Serena
t. +56 9 6685 8085
i. santorini_laserena

Along with their specialty seafood, **Mar Adentro (45)** regularly have live music and karaoke in their spacious place by the beach. Open all year. ◆$$$◆

a. Rengo 4629, La Serena
t. +56 9 6197 6978
w. maradentrorestaurant.cl

Tololo (46) is a bit of a fancier option; with its chic décor and artistic use of lighting it's a pretty-city-style restaurant on the beach - a fine spot to treat yourself to beautifully presented dishes from a choice of 3 menus. Snazzy. Open all year. ◆$$$◆ ◆$$$$◆

a. Avenida del Mar 5200, La Serena
t. +56 51 224 2656
w. tololo.cl

If you're off exploring up the Elqui Valley, find popular **Restaurant El Bosque Horcón (47)** in the mountains with an assortment of rustic dining areas set in the woods, in and amongst trees and natural water features. The magical spot is as well-known for the food as the atmosphere they've created with little wooden walkways, bridges and handmade benches dotted around the surrounds. Traditional local ingredients, served with style. They've cabins if you want to stay overnight. Open all year. ◆$$◆ ◆$$$◆

a. Horcón Bajo s/n, Valle de Elqui
t. +56 9 9531 3856
i. elbosque.restaurante

Colorful vintage style, quirky, full of curiosities and bric a brac, and a popular choice with locals and visitors alike, **La Delfina (48)** is the place to stop for a feed around Totoralillo. Servings are generous, food's tasty, people friendly, and they also have a little store selling sweets and restored furniture. Open all year. ◆$$◆ ◆$$$◆

a. Las Casas, Totoralillo
t. +56 9 7985 0697
i. ladelfina_restaurant

A 10-minute drive from Totoralillo, restobar **Sunset Las Tacas (49)** has white sand to the front, green garden to the rear and palm trees in between. Portions aren't the biggest we've ever seen but are fresh and full of flavor. The terrace is the place to be seen in summer - for lunch, dinner and drinks - so best to make a reservation. Open all year.

a. Las Tacas
t. +56 9 5343 4549
i. sunset_las_tacas

SHOP
◆

La Recova Municipal Market (50) was built more than a century ago and has long been considered the heart of La Serena. Here you can find pretty much everything spread over the two floors: Alpaca wools and woolens, stone crafts and carvings, pottery, jewelry, dried fruits, fresh fruits and veg, local and regional products. In typical South American style, the

market is chaotic, messy and dirty looking but bursting with life. Open daily except Sundays, all year round.

a. Cienfuegos 563, La Serena
t. +56 51 221 3888

If you haven't yet tried papayas en La Serena - the classic fruit of the region - here's the opportunity to get some fresh from the growers themselves. Run by the family Yanez, the **Papayas Yanez (51)** store can be found just 15 minutes' drive east of La Serena (direction Elqui Valley) and is filled with all things papaya, from fresh frutas to juice, oil, sweets, nectar and preserves. And cheeses too. Along with some other surprises. They've a big parking lot and offer tastings of most delicacies (within reason - don't expect a free brunch!). Open all year.

a. Km 11 Ruta 41, La Serena
t. +56 9 3095 3833
i. papayasyanez

SLEEP

Sleeping up to 4 persons, the domos on stilts just outside of town look especially impressive when they're all solar lit up inside at night. Each on its own platform with terrace, bbq and seating area with canopy, the **Domos Kunza Kamanchacos (52)** have a wooden walkway leading down to the white sand beach they sit above. Domos are comfortably furnished, with own private shower room, water dispenser, fridge, Bluetooth radio, and hairdryer. Luxuries! Communal areas in the Tourist Complex (also in domes) include a games room, children's play area and dining area. Open all year.
◆$$◆ ◆$$$◆

a. Punta de Choros
t. +56 9 6845 4729
w. domoskunzakamanchacos.cl

We love a small-scale place with personal touches, pet-friendly and all made with love. Find all that right on the beach at **Ekos de Mar (53)**

lodgings - cabanas and chiringuito - just 5 minutes south of Punta de Choros. A hearty breakfast is included with your stay and the beach bar serves delicious plates for lunch and dinner - local products, daily catch, home-baked goodies, refreshing beverages. If you're lucky you might even get to try their beer made from desalinated ocean water. The ideal only-the-sound-of-the-sea (and a few fellow guests) place to kick back and eat, sleep, surf/swim/snooze on the beach, repeat, for as long as you need to. Cabins sleep from 2 to 5 persons, facilities are basic but clean, best to book ahead. Open all year. ◆$$◆

a. Playa Las Conchitas, Punta de Choros
t. +56 9 9657 1439
i. ekosdemar

Converted colonial house in the center, **Hostal Maria Casa (54)** is a good option if you're on a budget. They've 9 rooms with private bathrooms, apartments sleeping from 2 to 6 persons, and a pretty little garden with a BBQ area, picnic tables and parasols. Within walking distance of the beach. Open all year. ◆$◆

a. Las Rojas 18, La Serena
t. +56 9 7466 7433
fb. Hostal Maria Casas

Hostal El Punto (55) is a cozy homely place with a nice atmosphere, run by the German owners, who long dreamed of creating a hub for travelers from all over the world to meet. They began renovating the colonial-style house in the center of La Serena in 2001, and opened their colorful hostel to guests in 2002. Breakfast is one of the highlights, they've also a cafeteria and bar, laundry room and relaxing garden. Open all year. ◆$$◆

a. Andres Bello 979, La Serena
t. +56 9 9627 9333
w. hostalelpunto.cl

Nothing fancy but cute, clean, well equipped and comfortable lodgings can be found close to the picturesque beach at **Totoralillo Casas y Cabañas (56)**. Owner Jessica will welcome you warmly and do her best to make sure you enjoy your stay, and you can save on parking charges by walking the kilometer and a bit to the beach. Bonus! Open all year. ◆$$◆

a. Totoralillo
t. +56 9 4653 3830
fb. Totoralillo Casas y Cabañas Thania

The last town on the coast of the Coquimbo region, Pichidangui offers some sheltered bays as well as a long stretch of beach popular with kite and windsurfers. Find **Bed & Wheels (57)** in the middle of the bay in an enclosed area with trees, swimming pool, children's area, wifi and secure parking. The super set-up for motorhomes / RVs was the idea of Jose Miguel Packziar and Jorge Ruddoff, after years of traveling in their own mobile homes wishing they could find a place to stay that met US standards. Clean and organized, with 20 sites connected to electricity, water and drainage facilities for campervans, they also have 6 fully equipped 2-bedroom cabanas that sleep up to 5. Open all year. ◆$$◆

a. Camino Santa Ines - Sitio 1, Pichidangui
t. +56 9 7801 1137
w. bedandwheels.cl

SURF

Along the oceanside of this region you'll find white sandy beaches, Caribbean-blue water and consistent surf. Although prone to wind, this stretch offers surfable options year-round. Visit in spring and you'll see desert flowers abloomin', and you can expect it to be pretty busy during summer. Like in the north - errr, yes we're in the north, but we mean the more northern north - the weather's agreeable in every season, as are the water temperatures. Wearing a 3.2 in summer, maybe with booties, should be doable.

PORTOFINO (I)

Portofino attracts a growing number of holidaymakers, hikers and bird watchers. Its waves and crystal-clear water obviously attract quite some number of surfers too. Along the

coastal road to **Chañaral** you can usually see waves rolling in. There are several line-ups which work best with a N swell. **Portofino** is a small set-up with a few very humble holiday houses and even fewer shops selling some basic essentials, and it's home to Portofino Surf Camp. There are also two natural sea pools that are safe for swimming. ◆ *Intermediate and advanced/rocks (and watch out for urchins)/surf school/easy parking.* ◆

CALDERA (II)

The area around **Bahía Inglesa** and

port city **Caldera** offers spots aplenty, with small beaches and inlets all about. A few are local competition sites; like **Playa Los Pulpos** (of the Pulpo Pro), north of Caldera. Most of these spots require an intermediate to advanced level of surfing but you can find beginner-friendly waves (and a mobile surf school) on small swell days at Playa Los Pulpos and **Playa Ramada**. Because of the many different bays, nooks and crannies, facing this way or that, there's always a wave to be found - depending on tide, wind, swell and swell direction.

HUASCO (III)

♦

Between Caldera and Huasco lie a few gems. Advanced surfers may want to check rocky lefthander **La Vedette** when big S or SW swells make other spots unsurfable. Find easier access and waves for all levels at **Tres Playitas** just to the north of Huasco, and exposed **Playa Brava** to the south of Huasco. A boat trip to **Isla Dama** is nice enough without having surf on your mind, but if you do, pick a SW swell day that may reward you with a clean reef break and flappy applause from the local sea lions - just make sure to give them some respectful space.

LA SERENA (IV)

♦

North of La Serena are some intermediate lefts and a right that you probably find easier to check out after

befriending someone from the small fishing community. Local fishermen are generally the best-informed people to talk to anyway, when it comes to waves, tides and access points.

The stretch of beach along La Serena's Avenida del Mar serves up waves for all levels and is crowded in summer. **El Faro** (also known as 'Poisson' - after the Poisson Surf School & Café) works throughout the tides but is usually better towards high. ♦ *All levels/ sand/shower/toilet/restaurant/surf shop/surf school/easy parking.* ♦

TOTORALILLO (V)

♦

Summer resort and popular surf village Totoralillo - referred to as Toto by locals - and its surroundings offer surf for sure: from big wave and barreling to easygoing and welcoming. The little headland jutting out to sea has spots that handle swells from different directions. When it's working, watch big wave riders at **El Cacho** (experts only). **El Muro** and **Pipe** are advanced spots, whereas the beach at **Derecharcha** is perfect for beginners. There's a surf school, showers and toilet, and parking's easy. At the small town of Pichidangui, south of Totoralillo, you can also find an all-level sandy beach, popular with kiters and windsurfers.

SCHOOL RENTAL SHOP

Stay, book a lesson, or rent your gear at **Portofino Surf Camp** (**58**). Run by the two surfing brothers Rodolfo and Nicolas, you'll be in the best of hands. They're conveniently close to a consistent righthand wave - in the land of the lefts! Open all year.

- **a.** Ruta C-260, Portofino
- **t.** +56 9 8267 0901
- **i.** portofinosurfcamp

You'll find mobile **Escuela de Surf Caldera** (**59**) at surf spots Pulpo or Rodillo in the Caldera area. The owner, Mauro Di Gino, is a well-known local surfer who knows his beaches, so if conditions require a different spot, they move there. On offer: lessons for every level, equipment rentals and surf essentials in their Caldera Surf Shop. Open all year.

- **a.** Caldera
- **t.** +56 9 4589 4117
- **fb.** Escuela de Surf Caldera

Find **Escuela de Surf Poisson** (**60**) along La Serena's seaside road, facing the town's main break. Owner Fernando is one of the pioneers in surf teaching in this area, with some 40 years of know-how under his belt. Book a single lesson or a course, rent equipment or find your essentials at their surf shop. There are also surf skate lessons on the menu. Open all year.

- **a.** Avenida Del Mar 1100, La Serena
- **t.** +56 9 9936 4753
- **i.** escuelasurfpoisson

Escuela de Surf Totoralillo (**61**) is located at the foot of tiny Totoralillo peninsula, a little south of Coquimbo. Besides surf lessons, they rent out SUP and surf equipment. Being enthusiastic climbers, they also offer bouldering classes, so you can explore the area's rocky places with them too. The owners of the school are environmentally and socially driven and were one of the early initiators of a clean and safe Totoralillo beach. Together with a local animal aid organization, they also help animals that are abandoned on the beach. Oh, sweet angels! Go visit them even if there's no surf here today, save a pup, clean a beach, why don't you… Open all year.

- **a.** Totoralillo
- **t.** +56 9 9741 6149
- **w.** surftotoralillo.cl

STRETCHING THE SIDE BODY: VIPARITA VIRABHADRASANA

◆

Reverse Warrior Pose

When your upper body feels tight, this pose is a nice mixture of strengthening and stretching.

Benefits:
Besides improving spinal mobility and opening the hips, this big side body stretch relieves tightness in the chest, helping to prevent risk of injury. Improves leg and core strength, and balance too.

How:
Start in a wide legged pose, turn your right foot out and left foot slightly in, then bend the right knee. As you inhale, reach the right arm up and over your head, while sliding the left hand down your left leg (don't put your weight on it though) - use your core to lift both sides of your upper body, create space and avoid sagging by keeping the pelvis straight. Engage the muscles in both legs, squeezing the right glute helps keep your knee aligned above your ankle. Stay here for a few breaths, then change sides.

IN AND AROUND LOS MOLLES, ZAPALLAR AND MAITENCILLO

♦

The northern part of the Valparaíso coast's commonly referred to as Costa Esmeralda but though the emerald-colored, crystalline water looks ever so inviting to go for a swim, its temperatures will likely make some body parts shrinkle, other parts screaming 'ayuda!' at the same time. (As in, your mickey shrinks to the point it resembles pinky-sized purple dried-up fox poo, and nipples hold bystanders at gunpoint, while threatening to explode.) But suited-up snorkeling, diving and suchlike ocean-time's highly recommended; you'll find diving schools aplenty in almost every seaside town you come upon.

While the translucent ocean, pelicans and other sea birds are an awe-inspiring constant, the coastal towns and settlements couldn't be more different. From lively Papudo, where Santiago families come for weekends and summers, to extrelegant Zapallar where the elite crew frolic on the promenade, and from laidback surf town Maitencillo to fishing bay Horcón-near-Puchuncaví where hippies came and went (although some stayed) leaving behind some happy-go-lucky vibes, and then to the only nudist beach in the country, Playa Luna.

Hopping from town to town, passing pine forests, nature reserves, surf spots, high cliffs and green hills, you'll find some fab places to while some time.

TO DO

♦

The **Reserva Puquén (1)** is a 200 hectare, privately owned nature reserve along the coast, open to the public. The park consists mainly of native flora, and the best season to witness what that looks like in full bloom is spring. You'll see migratory birds as well as native birds, and chinchillas - the fluffy-round-looking rodents - are common too. Explore on foot or bike, there are several routes, varying from 1 to 5 hours, trails are signposted. We can recommend the relatively short trek (approximately 1 hour walking) to the rock formation Salto el Puquén. Puquén in the local language means 'whale blow' or 'blowhole' (the waves that kaboom up between the rocks and high into the sky resemble a whale's explosive breath when it comes up for air). Every trail has viewpoints, try spot the sea lions that live on the little island 'Lobera' just off the coast. Open all year, Wednesday to Sunday.

a. El Lúcumo, Los Molles
t. +56 9 2239 6837
i. reservapuquen

The outdoor-loving peeps of **Intemperie Turismo (2)** offer about everything and anything alfresco, active and adventurous in the greater surroundings of Papudo. They'll take you on fun expeditions, from day trips by boat or kayak, to birdwatching or a sunset hike up the canyon Quebrada El Francés. Their guides are incredibly well informed, big on conservation, and keen to share their knowledge and experience of local history, nature, point out small details and grander views. Open all year, by reservation.

a. Avenida Irarrázaval, Playa Chica, Papudo
t. +56 9 7750 6305 / 9 8986 6131
w. intemperieturismo.cl

Find **Astromelia Spa (3)** halfway between Papudo and Zapallar, amid

pine forest, their treatment rooms open to ocean views. A wonderful place to relax, the only stress you might get is choosing which treatment to opt for: hydrotherapy, a facial or massage, aromatherapy, and then there are infrared saunas and hot tubs too. Feeling so sleepy and relaxed, or mesmerized by this little piece of paradise you don't want to travel any further? Ask if they've their dreamy wooden and stone cabins available to spend the night. Open all year, by reservation.

a. Along the F-30, Zapallar
t. +56 9 9323 9750
w. astromeliaspa.cl

People watch, bird watch (pelicans!), dolphin watch and drool over the

desirable mansions of the very-well-to-do in ritzy seaside town **Zapallar (4)**. It's easily explored on foot, its rambla, stone walkway, winding down to a secluded white sand beach. The rambla continues in both directions along the rocky coastline, both paths leading up to small headlands embracing the bay. From here you can look back at the surrounding hills, dotted with stunning villas, built in all sorts of styles. Rather check out the bay from the water, but braving the cold sea in your swimsuit's a bit too challenging?

Rent a kayak or SUP from **Kayak Zapallar (5)** or join one of their guided tours. Open all year.

a. Caleta Zapallar, Zapallar
t. +56 9 6494 2904
fb. kayakzapallar

Get all gooey-eyed observing the colony of penguins at **Isla Los Pinguinos Cachaguas (6)**. The Magellan and Humboldt Penguins are endangered species, and the island's a protected natural environment, but visitors are allowed to bypass the island by kayak or little boat. As long as no one is disturbing. But then again, we reckon they're quite easily disturbed, and you can simply watch the large colony from the beach of Cachagua. There are over 2000 of the noisy, awkwardly-moving little feathered ones, and the island also attracts sea otters and sea lions.

a. Playa Cachagua, Cachagua

Serene and stunning little **Playa las Cujas (7)** can be found at the northern end of Cachagua. The inlet's protected from the Atlantic swells, it's perfect if you're looking for calmer and turquoise waters to swim or snorkel, and safe for children who'll be happy splashing around in natural rockpools and puddles, finding shells, starfish and crabs. Gets busy easily in summer because of its tiny size. Either walk from the car park along Avenida del Mar down to the beach, or hike along the coast from Cachagua (wearing some sensible shoes!).

a. Playa las Cujas, Avenida del Mar 524, Cachagua

Lagunita (8) wellness center's kinda that and a bit more - best described as a creative and active hub, vibing fun, magic and connection. What to expect? A bike pump track and climbing wall for youngsters, daily

yoga and dance workshops, a gym, co-working spaces (which you can rent for anything from an hour to a month), a bar and a restaurant. On top of that they've a veg garden and brew their own beer! Find them just outside Maitencillo inland of the estuary, turn right off the E-46 (direction Catapilco) at the entrance to Parque Cachagua and turn right again towards Baldén (estuary). Open all year.

a. La Laguna
t. +56 9 9332 2062
w. lagunita.cl

Del Mar Park (9) have skate ramps and a skate pool, open for all levels. They offer group and individual lessons, organize beach clean-ups and host festivals, and there's a restaurant and surf school too. Open all year.

a. Playa El Abanico Norte, Sector 4, Avenida Del Mar 24, Maitencillo
t. +56 9 7734 1980
w. delmarpark.cl

EAT/DRINK/HANG OUT
◆

Empanadas aplenty, wherever you go in Chile. We recommend **Empanadas El Mellizo (10)** because of their variety and use of ingredients that will also please vegetarian and vegan aficiona-

dos. Besides empanadas, they've fries and burgers to-go. Open in summer. ♦$♦

a. In front of Playa Chica, Papudo
i. empanadaselmellizo

Popular with all and every one, including the famous, **El Chiringuito** (**11**) is a traditional restaurant serving seafood. It's pricey, but the location overlooking the ocean is stupendous, and their wine list goes on forever. Chances to spot a national or even international star or starlet are included in the service (the latter being very unofficial and complaints about not catching sight of a famous face forking a crustacean-filled platter can be directed to our complaints department). Open all year, making a reservation is highly recommended. ♦$$$♦

a. Francisco de Paula Perez, Zapallar
t. +56 33 274 1024

Located right on the beach, no prize for guessing that restaurant **Nuevo Cesar** (**12**) serves seafood, but it's also a pretty desirable spot to go for morning drinks, or simply enjoy a sunset cocktail and people-watch. Open all year. ♦$$$♦

a. Avenida Zapallar 177, Zapallar
t. +56 9 5880 4499
fb. Nuevo Cesar Zapallar

Grab a coffee and some finger-licking tasty torta (cake) at cafetería and pastelería **Emporio Don Matias** (**13**). The friendly family-run café offers brunch, tostadas, quiches, salads and wraps too. Open all year. ♦$$♦

a. Avenida Cachagua 288, Cachagua
t. +56 9 6468 8907
i. emporiodonmatias

El Hoyo Maitencillo (**14**) is a popular beachside bar and restaurant. Usually quite busy, though their large wooden decked terrace offers enough space and overlooks the ocean. On the menu, the usual tasty Chilean goods: seafood and empanadas. Open all year. ♦$$♦

a. Avenida del Mar 1060, Puchuncaví, Maitencillo
t. +56 32 277 2355
i. elhoyomaitencillo

Pizzería Mónaco (15) are best known for their pizza bases made with the famous Masa Madre - Chile's traditional fermented equivalent to sourdough. And they serve salads, ceviche and plant-based options too. Choose to sit inside or outside, there's a fire burning on cold days. Open all year. ♦$$♦

a. Avenida Del Mar 1408, Puchuncaví, Maitencillo
t. +56 9 4490 5073
i. monaco.maitencillo

From the terrace of restaurant, surf school and shop **Beach House Maitencillo (16)** you've a front-row view of the waves at Playa Aguas Blancas. They serve an excellent cuppa, cakes, tostadas, and have a skate ramp on the premises. No wonder it's a favorite hangout for locals and visitors alike. Open all year. ♦$♦ ♦$$♦

a. Avenida Del Mar 3804, Puchuncaví, Maitencillo
t. +56 9 8505 9524
i. beachouse.maitencillo

SHOP
◆

If you like the smell of incense, **Flor de la Vida (17)** might just be the place for you to hunt for bohemian-style home décor, jewelry, or finding a little something to sparkle up your spiritual path, like precious stones and symbolic items. Most products are handmade, lovingly curated and sought out by the owner on his travels to Southeast Asia. And the incense is for sale too! Open all year.

a. Avenida Del Mar 1019, Maitencillo
t. +56 9 9735 6122
i. flordelavidatienda

Surf and outdoor lifestyle store **Santas Pecadoras (18)**, owned and run by fun loving and knowledgeable chicas, sells a variety of quality clothing brands, accessories, surf essentials and beach needs. Open all year.

a. Avenida Central 1045 N L6, Maitencillo
t. +56 9 9772 7797
i. santaspecadoras

Find children's, ladies and unisex apparel, and unique handmade jewelry at **Manada (19)**. For those tending to lose or forget their sunglasses often (guilty!), we recommend checking their stylish straps, or maybe opt for one of their sun hats or caps. Open all year.

a. Avenida Del Mar 1019, Maitencillo
t. +56 9 9705 0967
i. manada.tienda

You might've noticed that pretty much everything in Maitencillo revolves around the beach and the Avenida Del Mar, activities, restaurants, shops - ever so easy. At **Feria Artesanal Maitencillo (20)**, along the same avenida, you'll find some small shops and galleries selling crafts, art, jewelry and more. Open all year.

a. Avenida Del Mar 506, Maitencillo

SLEEP
◆

Family and surfer friendly **Camping Chivato (21)** is set beautifully along the ocean with shaded pitches for tents and beachside parking for campervans. Besides designated places for tents and vans they've domos (dome shaped cabins), family cabins, and cabins sleeping 2. There's a café on the premises. Open all year. ♦$♦ ♦$$♦

a. Ruta 5 S km 186, Los Molles
t. +56 9 9934 4651
w. campingchivato.cl

Find tranquil **Chanagua Lodge (22)** at the northern end of Playa Los Molles. They've comfy rooms with terraces facing the sea. They offer all sorts

of activities in the surroundings, like diving excursions and apnea training, guided trips to Tesoro del Pangal Ecological Reserve, or hikes in Reserva Puquén. On site, you can book yoga classes, massages, and even a Tarot card reading. Their restaurant serves wholesome and healthy meals. Open all year. ◆$$$◆

a. Los Pescadores 1451, Los Molles
t. +56 9 4685 6873
w. chanagua.com

Have Brad Pitt giving you a lap dance or hang out with some of his other purring pals at cat-friendly **Hostal Maitencillo Norte (23)** (yeah, sorry, Brad's a cat). Find them chilling on the couch or join them and your fellow travelers lounging in the garden together at night, fairy lights overhead. There'll undoubtedly be someone strumming a guitar, and you'll be sharing drinks and stories with guests from all over the world. Write your name on the wall before you leave, and try spot how many names from your home country you recognize. Besides cats with cool names, they've private and shared bedrooms. Leave your ride in the private parking for the rest of your stay and set out on foot - the beach and all other amenities are within walking distance. Open all year. ◆$◆ ◆$$◆

a. Ricardo 134, Maitencillo
t. +56 9 8832 6908
i. hostalmaitencillonorte

Surrounded by a lavish green garden, posada (guesthouse) **Portal del Sol** (24) sits just steps away from Playa Aguas Blancas. The use of wood and glass give the guesthouse a spacious feel, the décor is a tastefully curated collection of items from around the world, the owners nonetheless doing a marvelous job creating a homely atmosphere. Every room depicts a place or land, subtle details defining its theme. There's bright and light 'Toscana', sophisticated use of blue and white in 'Greca', and 'Marraquech' has a dreamy, yet sturdy Moroccan vibe. Open all year. ◆$$◆

a. Vista Hermosa s/n Cerro Tacna, Maitencillo
t. +56 9 9338 3590
i. portaldelsol.maitencillo

IN AND AROUND VALPARAÍSO AND VIÑA DEL MAR

This area of the coast's a very popular (and populated) section, much visited by both Chileans and international tourists. The historic quarter of seaport Valparaíso is a World Heritage Site, selected by UNESCO for its 19th-century urban architecture, adapted to the steep hillsides, flowered with church spires and numerous funicular elevators (cable cars).

As one of Chile's biggest port cities, some neighborhoods of Valparaíso are a bit rough - if you pass through one of the slums, you'd best drive with your doors locked and won't want to leave your vehicle unattended. Suffice to say, these pockets lack the vibe of a touristy destination, but drive on to the hilly colorful old part and find streets decorated with one-of-a-kind artwork, filled with sparkling energy, edgy creativity and a postcard prettiness that's outstandingly unique. This is where you want to park your ride (still don't leave valuables inside, though eh!) and get lost exploring the steep little roads, stop to admire street art and take in great views over the multicolored roofs in each of its picturesque corners. Valparaíso is where cultural heritage meets the 21st century, as colonial Victorian buildings now host hipster rooftop bars. You'll discover something new in 'Valpo' each time you visit.

Right next door, twin city Viña del Mar (Vineyard of the Sea) is commonly called Viña and often referred to as La Ciudad Jardín (The Garden City). Once part of Valparaíso and in the Valparaíso Region, you'd expect more similarity in the two cities' styles, however, few of the 19th-century buildings of Viña survived a series of earthquakes in the 1800s. But it's well known for its buzzing beaches, resorts, parks and gardens, especially in the summer months of January and February.

If you're looking for less of a cosmopolitan vibe and more surf breaks and holiday-residence style, check out nearby coastal towns like Reñaca, Concón and Ritoque. While Reñaca's hollow beach break makes it perfect for Chilean surf tournaments, Concón (La Boca) is more suited to beginner and intermediate surfers, and Ritoque has all the California feels. This is where the story of surfing began in Chile, back in the seventies, and since then nothing much has changed - where the almost untouched, great long dune-backed beach makes the crowds that you left behind in traffic a few minutes ago seem like nothing but a distant memory.

TO DO

◆

Surrounded by native forest, dunes and the extensive Humadal de Mantagua wetlands, **Playa Ritoque** (**25**) is a paradisical and quiet stretch of beach, just north of Concón. Making the little detour to get to this beach might leave you feeling this is not so much a To Do, but rather a To Be. Aside from a couple of beach restaurants, there aren't too many distractions. You might scare flocks of birds on the beach, perhaps wave at pelicans flying by, give some love to the stray dogs. In the surrounding dunes, wetlands and forest hides a variety of wildlife, migrating and native birds, mammals and reptiles. There's a wooden pedestrian bridge crossing the wetlands. You can also walk up to the rocks, then continue up the path at the north side of the beach. Try stretching your stay until the magical golden hour, when the sun's about to call it a day.

a. Playa Ritoque, Quintero

Although declared a nature sanctuary, the **Dunes of Concón** (**26**) are open to the public. You can hike up them and may see some locals sandboarding down their steep slopes. It can get pretty warm if the sun's out, so you might want to go early or later in the day, but the views are rewarding, as is the leg work! Find the dunes between Concón and Reñaca - it feels as though the two urbanized areas are slowly eating into this unique piece of land. Please be careful of the tiny shrubby plants on your way, they're in need of preservation just as much as the rest of the area. Open all year.

a. Concón

The epic **coastal drive along Avenida Borgoño** (**27**) between Concón and Viña del Mar offers views of turquoise water and amazing rock formations - if the weather allows. Just watch out for joggers on the side of the road. Traffic in January and February can be heavy but for the rest of the year it's a breeze. There's a worthy stop at viewpoint Roca Oceánica to stretch your legs and, err, take in the view from this point before you keep cruising. Open all year.

a. Avenida Borgoño, Concón

If you love green as much as blue, and the mountainside as much as the seaside, head inland from Viña del Mar to **La Campana National Park (28)**. Divided into 3 sections, the park covers 8000 hectares and was created in the late 1960s, with environmental conservation and sustainable tourism in mind. It's a grand opportunity to discover Central Chile's finest and most unique plants, trees - like the Chilean palm - birds and (little) beasts, and there's even a 30-meter high waterfall. You might spot an eagle flying overhead, or a Chilean mockingbird, or maybe feel the eyes of foxes and chinchillas spying on you. The best way to discover all beauty is to set out on foot. There are hiking trails for both hardcore (try the Granizo section, also if you're into climbing) and leisurely wanderers (you'll be happy to choose Cajón Grande). If you're keen to see the waterfall, opt for the Palmas de Ocoa section. There are picnic areas, and designated camping spaces for those who'd like to trek a few days. If you dare to hike up to the 1850-meter-high summit (approximately 8 hours, no access to the summit between June and August) you can walk in the footsteps of Charles Darwin, who made it to the top of Cerro La Campana in the 1800s. From here you can see both the Andes Mountains and the Pacific Ocean. Most trails are well marked, and you can ask the staff at the entrance desks for tips. From Limache (nearby Viña del Mar) there are direct buses running to the park, or opt for the taxis colectivos. Bring a day pack of water and food, and leave nothing but your footprints. Open all year.

a. Avenida Granizo, paradero 45 comuna de Olmué (Sector de Granizo) / Ruta 5 Norte Km 98 comuna de Hijuelas (Sector Palmas de Ocoa)
t. +56 33 244 3067
w. conaf.cl/parques/parque-nacional-la-campana

Viña's International Song Festival, the **Festival Internacional de la Canción de Viña del Mar (29)** is held in February each year and has been since 1960 (before Woodstock and Glastonbury were so much as a dream). Besides the contest, there are numerous live acts; international Hispanic artists such as Shakira, Julio Iglesias and Ricky Martin have all performed here over the years. Try spot and bet your pesetas on the next Ricky, Julio or hips that don't lie. Being part of 'El Monstruo', the monster, aka the audience, you also get a say in who wins a prize, in several categories.

a. Anfiteatro de la Quinta Vergara, Parque Quinta Vergara, Viña del Mar

We mentioned the street art of Valparaíso in the intro; if you truly want to learn all the ins and outs, the secrets and the fun stuff, the messages behind the murals, graffiti, the words, colors and tags, join the **Valpo Street Art Tours (30)**. They'll take you along to pieces that are not to be missed as well as the less obvious, tucked away in a corner, along stairs or some dark alley you almost certainly would've missed without a passionate and knowledgeable guide shining some light on them. It's also a safe way to enter some of the sketchier parts of town, where they work with local guides. You can book to join a group tour or a private tour with your own party. Available all year.

a. Valparaíso
t. +56 9 3248 5231
w. valpostreetart.com

La Sebastiana Museo de Pablo Neruda (31), one of the houses of Chilean politician and diplomat but above all poet, Pablo Neruda, has earned the status of National Monument and is open to the public. Neruda's easily one of the most important 20th-century poets, who dedicated much of his work to the charms of Latin America, and especially his home country, Chile. He won the International Peace prize in 1950, and the Nobel prize for literature in the early 1970s, but was also known for his rather eccentric character and taste in houses and their interiors. Colorful La Sebastiana sits on Florida Hill overlooking the city and the ocean - he preferred solitude but not too much of it. The house is named after its first owner, who never got to finish the remarkable construction. Inside, find all kinds of odd and quirky relics and objects and lots of old maps and seascapes. Open all year.

a. Ricardo de Ferrari 692, Valparaíso
t. +56 32 223 3759
w. fundacionneruda.org

Half an hour's drive from Valparaíso, **Laguna Verde (32)** (Green Lagoon) is a muy tranquilo town with little more than a salt lake, secluded beach and dense pine forest. Amazing raw nature, tranquility without the crowds and the not-so-cold-as-the-sea temperature of the lagoon is inviting for a swim. There's a viewpoint before reaching Laguna Verde, a few restaurant options and paid parking. Open all year.

a. Laguna Verde

EAT/DRINK/HANG OUT
◆

If you're after classic fried empanadas, **Las Deliciosas (33)** is where to find them! By no means healthy but packed with all the taste you need to alleviate any guilt you might have about that. As you savor the flavors, with cheese melting over and around a filling of fresh local seafood, we think you'll agree they're deliciosa for sure. Open all year. ◆$$◆

a. Avenida Borgoño 25370, Concón
t. +56 9 4145 4234
w. lasdeliciosas.cl

High in the hills of Concón, you might not expect much as you enter the traditional-looking restaurant from the street, but as you walk through **El Faro de los Compadres (34)** restaurant to the terrace and see the view from above the bay, take a sip of your pisco sour and the rest is history. Best known for its fish and seafood but they also serve a delightful Chilean vegan dish. Although we forgot the name (sorry), this rice dish is packed with veggies and full of flavor. Best to book ahead during high season and at weekends. Open all year. ◆$$◆

a. El Prado 2585, Concón
t. +56 32 281 5087
i. farodeloscompadres

Right across from Playa Reñaca, **Praia Sushi Reñaca (35)** is a small place serving freshly prepared portions that are sure to 'satisface tu apetito'! They've only a few streetside tables, so get a takeout if you prefer a beachside meal. Open all year. ◆$$◆

a. Avenida Borgoño 15588, Reñaca
t. +56 9 6399 7622
w. praiasushi.cl

Find trendy restaurant **El Patio (36)** serving tasty and healthy burritos and bowls, kombucha and the like. Their El Patio Café faces the beach, and El Patio Juice Bar is just round the corner in a small side street. Both use local ingredients in all their dishes wherever possible. The café includes a little concept store, where you'll find some sustainably made on-the-road essentials. Open all year. ◆$$◆

a. Avenida Ignacio Carrera Pinto 110, Reñaca
t. +56 9 4112 2721
w. elpatiocl.com

There's much more to **Green Lab (37)** than meets the eye. Founded in 2018 by two friends (a meat-loving Chilean and a vegan Brit) they blended their ideas to create Chile's first healthy fast food chain. Grab a menu and choose your base, protein, toppings and sauce, and within no time you'll be called for your custom-made tasty food. They're a well-known name in Santiago, but here's where they began, a stone's throw from the ocean. We love not only the delicious food and generous portions but also their story, vision and people. On a mission to give back to the area, Thomas, a local surfer, is working to build a circular economy into the roots of Green Lab - think growing their own veggies, compostable packaging, feeding leftover food to animals of local farmers, hosting beach cleans, reducing their footprint while making a positive impact. And the bigger they grow, the bigger their mission becomes! Our kinda people. Open all year. ◆$$◆

a. 8 Norte 404, Viña del Mar
t. +56 32 362 7724
w. greenlabchile.cl

To get into restobar **WineBox (38)** you need to ring the doorbell and say your name. Then hidden behind a

wall, you find what feels like a whole new world opening up for you - as the stairs take you up to the rooftop restaurant, you'll see the incredible view of the port and surrounding hills. On top of the tasty and affordable tapas, the atmosphere is tip-top too. If you decide to spend the night, you've the option to book one of their super stylish shipping containers turned into hipster hotel rooms (see Sleep section). Open every day for lunch, dinner and /or drinks, all year. Reservations recommended. ◆$$◆

a. Baquedano 763, Valparaíso
t. +56 9 5824 4497 / 9 6908 9224
fb. Winebox Valparaíso

SHOP

Rincón Natural (39) sell only healthy and nutritious goodness because, as they like to say, 'Let your medicine be your food and food your medicine.' Think

all your essentials, top up your grains, rice, nuts and nibbles in bulk, fresh fruit and veg, deli goodies, honey, daily baked sourdough (masa madre), eggs straight from the farm... And you can stop on the terrace for an almond milk latte before you leave. Open all year.

a. Avenida Concón Reñaca 360, Concón
i. elalimentotumedicina

From 15 Norte Street all the way to the Casino in Plaza Colombia, connecting the northern Valparaíso region to the south, about 2 kilometers of smooth flat sidewalks make Avenida San Martín the perfect playground for skateboarding in Viña del Mar. **Sanma Skate Shop (40)**, conveniently located along this very avenida, sells all skate essentials and lifestyle needs. You can also opt for skate lessons. Open all year.

a. Avenida San Martín 458, Local 14a, Viña del Mar
t. +56 9 9841 4037
w. sanmaskateshop.cl

Find Valparaíso's daily fresh market, **Mercado El Cardonal (41)**, set in a 1917 building, offering local produce like fruit, vegs, cheese, and much more. There are small eateries too, their staff eager to lure you in as their next customer. Open all year.

a. Uruguay 125, Valparaíso

Ápfel (42) is a Chilean swimwear brand that's unique in their designs, and they love to show how beautiful their swimsuits, bikinis and beachwear look on different sized bodies. Because, let's face it; beach life is for every body! Open all year.

a. Avenida Borgoño 14580 local 8A, Plaza Reñaca, Reñaca
t. +56 32 283 4619 / 9 3590 0679
w. apfel.cl

SLEEP
◆

As a child, Diego dreamed that one day he'd build a place in Ritoque for people who came to enjoy the beach all day to also be able to stay for the night. Many years, careers and stories later, he turned his dream into reality and created **La Ritoqueña (43)**. This beautiful wooden beach hotel with a whole lot of soul is only steps away from the surf, with a small cozy set-up and a most welcoming host, whose greatest pleasure is to make you feel at home. If the lounge area, complete with fireplace for any cold winter nights, isn't enough to relax you, then let Diego know (in advance) that you'd like to stay in for lunch or dinner and he'll prepare you an excellent meal with fresh-from-the-market produce. There's also a huge rooftop (yoga classes in summer!), and a hammock on each private balcony with a super-tastic view of palm trees and ocean. If you want to explore the beach and dunes, you can rent fat bikes from Diego. Open all year. ◆$$$◆ ◆$$$$◆

a. Ritoque Sitio 70, Quintero
t. +56 9 6121 2436
w. laritoquena.com

The owners of **Not Found Rooms (44)** have created a hostel with a snazzy vibe, light and spacious with lots of playful art, beautiful wooden floors and cool interior design. The bedrooms are bright and light too, with comfy beds, and you'll be energized for the day ahead after a plentiful fresh breakfast, which is included in your stay. Open all year. ◆$◆

a. Paseo Cousiño 12C, Viña del Mar
t. +56 9 3054 8854
i. notfoundrooms

If you're not already tempted to stay due to their location on the Cerro Alegre (Happy Hill) or their slogan 'Don't worry, be Maki', then check out the **Maki Hostel (45)** for its color, creativity and custom. As well as bringing all the best traits of Valparaíso inside, this beautiful old building has a wonderful view of the city's rooftops from the balcony, a sunny morning patio, and a green roof - created to cultivate their own veggies in the middle of the city. They've got double, family and bunk rooms so are suited to everyone from the solo traveler to couples, families and groups. Open all year. ◆$◆

a. Urriola 428, Valparaíso
t. +56 9 6749 3760
w. makihostels.com

A popular stay for backpackers, **Casa Volante Hostal** (**46**) feels more cozy little casa than hostel. Located in the middle of Valparaíso so you can step out of the door and straight into its buzzing energy. They've bunkrooms, private and shared, and lively communal spaces, including a bar. The house is run with love and a true community feeling, as well as a big effort to be as eco-efficient and friendly as possible. Also included in your stay; good internet, a varied breakfast buffet, secure lockers in shared rooms and a safe box at reception, table games and all the information and advice you could need on the city and what to do while you're there. Open all year. ◆$◆

a. Escalera Fischer 27, Valparaíso
t. +56 9 3191 7326
w. casavolantehostal.com

It's hard to miss **Winebox** (**47**) with its bold colors and iconic look. This funky and unique boutique apart-hotel jumps out from its surroundings on the hill with a pop. The clever and tasteful design started with 25 shipping containers - plenty of windows and portholes added - each room has a balcony with a harbor view and if you want a bit more panorama, head for the rooftop terrace bar. Owned by a now-local winemaker (originally from New Zealand) whose urban winery's also on location; offer to get involved if you've a desire to crush grapes, and you'll definitely find some wine in your mini fridge. Free secure underground parking for guests. Open all year. ◆$$$◆

a. Baquedano 763, Valparaíso
t. +56 9 5824 4497 / 9 6908 9224
fb. Winebox Valparaiso

In the mystical port of Valparaíso, at the foot of Cerro Barón and just four blocks from the main bus station, find **La Joya Hostel** (**48**). You can tell as you enter that this place was designed for the digital nomad. They have their own restaurant, bar, rooftop terrace and coworking space. If you need to combine your holiday travel time with some remote work, this place should tick all the boxes. Choose a private or shared room and enjoy a modern and comfortable Joya avant-garde experience. Open all year. ◆$◆

a. Quillota 80, Valparaíso
t. +56 9 3187 8552
w. lajoyahostel.com

Boutique hotel **Casa Puente** (**49**) is where art, culture and history combine in a restored iconic mansion. The architecture is typical for the area. Constructions like these were built by immigrants - mainly merchant mariners - who settled in the city in the late 19th century. Having been empty for more than a decade, the site was restored by the owners, working with renowned Chilean artists to design and decorate each room uniquely, creating the distinctive lodging experience of today. A delight to rest your head, and if you spot anything to your liking, or fall head over heels for them, you can obtain some of the art as well! There's a pool and a large terrace from where you've a view of the Valparaíso hills. To top it off, they host regular live music, art venues and theatre events at their café. Excited to sleep inside a work-of-art mansion in one of Chile's most artistic neighborhoods? Open all year, free parking. ◆$$$◆

a. Pasaje San Agustín 552, Valparaíso
t. +56 32 337 3801
w. casapuente.cl

IN AND AROUND ALGARROBO AND SANTO DOMINGO

◆

Heading south from Valparaíso city, the scenery changes drastically; concrete jungle becomes lush countryside, thickly forested and hilly. From the coastal town of Quintay all the way to Santo Domingo the rural landscape sets the pace of life, *con toda tranquilidad*.

You'll be driving along the Litoral de Los Poetas, the Coast of the Poets. Chilean poets and artists Pablo Neruda, Vicente Huidobro, Violeta Parra and Nicanor Parra were charmed off their feet and inspired by the surroundings, the seascapes and picturesque towns along this route, such as El Quisco, Isla Negra, Las Cruces, Cartagena, El Tabo and Algarrobo. You can spend at least a day following their traces (see To Do section).

During summer, these are hugely popular coastal towns, so you won't be alone - and that might be a slight understatement, it does get very busy - although Algarrobo, Quintay, Tunquén and Santo Domingo are a bit more exclusive and seemingly attract fewer crowds. The fact that the largest outdoor swimming pool in the world belongs to a private condo in Algarrobo may give you a rough idea of its high-end vibes.

There are several surf breaks along this coast where you'll find far more people on the beach than in the ocean. If you want to avoid the busy beaches altogether, best travel here outside of January and February.

The further south you travel, towards Santo Domingo, the crowds thin, even in high season. Hike up the winding roads of Las Rocas de Santo Domingo past large, traditional family houses with meticulously tended gardens. The building design in this area was inspired by the Palos Verde resort in California, because of its similar climate and landform, so you may feel strangely like you've been picked up and plonked down far north of Chile.

TO DO

◆

The tiny fishing village of Quintay was once home to the country's largest whaling station - where whales where processed and used for soap, meat, oil, grease and all manner of other products. This was also common practice in other seaside towns until the seventies, when (luckily, we say) they stopped operating. Nowadays whale hunting is banned off Chile's coast but you can visit the **Museo Ex Ballenera (50)** to learn about the region's somewhat brutal whaling history and the reasons for later proclaiming their waters a whale sanctuary. Dedicated to creating awareness about the role of marine mammals and the protection of coastal life, the museum's run by the Fundación Quintay and is open all year from Thursday to Sunday.

a. Caleta de Quintay, Quintay
t. +56 32 236 2511
w. fundacionquintay.com

Casablanca Valley is only a small part of the larger wine region Aconcagua but (how convenient for us ocean addicts) only 30 kilometers from the coast. The relatively warm and dry area benefits from the proximity of the cooling ocean breezes. If you want to dive into the notes and afternotes, colors, body, acidity, tannins, textures and whatnots of this region's wines - Chardonnay, Sauvignon Blanc, Pinot Noir, Syrah - there are plenty of wineries that open their cellar doors for tastings, tours and shopping. In the Rosario Valley, close to coastal towns Las Cruces and San Sebastián, **Matetic Vineyards (51)** deserve a special mention for being pioneers in using earth-friendly biodynamic methods to produce their wines. While sampling their goods, you can learn about biodynamic wine-making, step-by-step. Unable to make it back to the coast due to over-sampling? They've an on-site restaurant and boutique hotel too. Open all year.

a. Fundo el Rosario, San Antonio, Casablanca
t. +56 2 2611 1501
w. matetic.com

In need of a slice of solitude? The two-kilometer-long, white sand **Playa Tunquén (52)** provides; with access to it via the dunes working wonders as a 'crowd filter'. From the car park (paid parking), it takes some 20 minutes hiking along a beautiful trail before you reach the beach. You'll see unique plants, horses grazing and all kinds of birdlife. Tunquén in Mapudungun (Chile's native language) means as much as 'land that cracks or opens up'. See for yourself just how apt the name is. The surrounding area's refreshingly underdeveloped - you'll spot a few summer houses (all solar powered) in the surrounding dunes, most of them owned by Chilean celebrities and politicians seeking privacy. Always keep an eye on the waves, maybe something will come rolling your way. Ah, but then you have to hike all the way back to get your board! And beware of strong undercurrents, swimming's not recommended.

a. Playa Tunquén, Algarrobo

Entering Hostal La Tabla you might wonder whether this is a bouldering hall, hostel, shop, coffee stop, or functional training studio of sorts. Well, it's a bit of everything. Amicable owner Francisco Puelles, better known as 'Chapu', built **Zona Boulder (53)** inside his hostel. An avid and stoked climber (and surfer) himself, Chapu will be happy to help you climb the wall. Open all year.

a. Avenida La Montaña 0721, El Quisco
t. +56 9 9698 3240
i. zona.boulder

As mentioned before in the Valparaíso section, you've a few options to visit one of the houses-turned-into-museums of Chile's most famous and beloved poet Pablo Neruda. He owned 3 houses, but **Casa Museo Isla Negra**

(**54**) was his favorite, where he spent the last years of his life and did most of his writing. The ocean, an endless inspiration in his poems and stories, is notably present in the house; from the unobstructed view of the sea crashing onto an assembly of black rocks (hence the name) to the artifacts such as seashells, whale teeth, ship replicas and ships in bottles. Open all year.

a. Pasaje Gonzalito, Isla Negra, El Quisco
w. fundacionneruda.org

While we're on the subject; you might want to further follow the **Litoral de Los Poetas (55)** (Coast of the Poets). From Isla Negra, continue south along the seaside to the next town, Las Cruces, where the so-called anti-poet and creative Nicanor and his artist sister, Violeta Parra, lived and worked. Their house is not open to the public, but the surrounding streets are free to wander and wonder where they found their inspiration. Further south, in Cartagena, you can visit the Decorative Arts Villa Lucia, which was the house of writer and painter Adolfo Couve, and the museum of Vicente Huidobro, a contemporary poet. While this area used to be an artist's magnet, the towns have lost some of their allure and some critics say there's very little being done to keep the poetry alive - no writing festivals, poetry slams or events celebrating the written word. We say, judge for yourself, and all the while enjoy the landscape, the light and sea views that attracted the poets

in the first place. Just be aware the months of January and February are very busy. Open all year.

a. Litoral de Los Poetas,
   Ruta del Mar (G-98-F)

At Chépica beach in El Tabo you can have some fun with your skateboard at **Rampa Limpia (56)**. The name means ´Clean Ramp´ and is for good reason - the skate area doubles as a recycling spot, and the small fee you pay for using the ramp is used to promote local initiatives such as beach cleaning and free sports workshops for the community. Our kinda spot. Open all year.

a. Playa Chépica, El Tabo
i. rampalimpia

Join a **yoga class (57)** with an ocean view, just 5 steps from the beach (we counted) on the wooden deck of restaurant Santa Pizza. If it gets too windy, the class will take place inside, where the floor-to-ceiling windows won't obstruct your view of the sea. Open all year, classes on demand.

a. Paseo del Mar 140, Santo Domingo
t. +56 9 8818 5585
i. santapizzacl

The drive down the lush valley into nature reserve **Parque Tricao (58)** to the lake below offers a different view with every turn you take. Once there, you can park your car and set out on foot. The paths are well maintained and easy to follow. Besides hiking, there are more activities on offer, like kayaking, bird watching and boat tours. There's an MTB circuit, and a large, adventurous and fun playground for younger children, made entirely out of natural materials. You can bring a picnic (and please take all leftovers and trash back with you) and maybe some binoculars too! There's a 2-hectare aviary (with special nets, allowing bees and other insects to flit freely in and out) that houses over 800 birds - you can watch them from viewpoints, connected by trails and wooden suspension bridges. The park is an initiative run by a non-profit organization focused on the preservation of native flora and fauna. By keeping the park open to the public, and offering recreational and educational activities, they hope future generations can still enjoy the great outdoors too. The park also has a restaurant, pets aren't allowed in the park. Open all year, you can purchase tickets in advance.

a. Avenida Las Brisas, Santo Domingo
w. tricao.cl

For more hiking, bird watching and into-the-wild feel, head further south to **Reserva Nacional El Yali (59)**. The 520 hectares of wetland and untouched nature are home to some 115 bird species. There are 3 areas open to the public - you can spend at least half a day per area (on foot). Open all year, contact the park's office 48 hours before arrival.

a. El Convento, Santo Domingo
t. +56 35 244 2772
w. conaf.cl/parques/reserve-nacional-el-yali

EAT/DRINK/HANG OUT

Not only the best (woodfire) pizza in town - in our humble opinion - you'll also find the atmosphere at **Pizzeria El Templo (60)** makes you feel like you belong to their little free-spirited community, even for a short lunch or dinner break. The terrace sits within a wooden fenced garden with an orchard, where you can keep an eye on the outdoor oven as your order's heating up, cheese melting, crust getting crunchier. Vegan options, pastas, salads, fresh juices and desserts are on offer too. They regularly have live music and a campfire on weekends. Find them just off the main street. Open all year: daily in high season, weekends

only the rest of the year. ♦$$♦

a. Los Almendros 751, Quintay
t. +56 9 4545 1659
w. eltemplo.cl

Another eatery much to our liking in Quintay is **Caleté (61)**. The small restaurant has a wooden terrace looking out to sea, and you'll experience a local vibe here for sure. The owners work directly with the pescadores from the fishermen's union of Quintay, so bona fide local and freshly prepared and served. We recommend trying the Congrio and the Locos with mayo. Open all year, seasonal opening hours can vary. ♦$$♦

a. Avenida Costanera 92, Caleta Quintay, Quintay
t. +56 9 5016 1904
i. calete_quintay

Enjoy the sea breeze and some sun on your face, listening to the birds singing while drinking your coffee at **Dulce Avenida Coffee (62)**. If you've been craving something sweet, the dulce in their name provides - the cakes are irresistible. Ask Fabi, who serves the goods, for local tips on what to do and where to go, and she'll happily share some. Open all year. ♦$$♦

a. Avenida Carlos Alessandri 280, Algarrobo
t. +56 9 8388 3467
i. dulceavenida

Koru Quiosco (63) has a panoramic view of the Algarrobo coast and surf break Tinajas. It's one of the few classic beach kiosks left along this coast, but they're pretty newfangled in being plastic-free and having veggie and vegan options on offer too. They've beach items, such as umbrellas, for rent, a little library and serve as a touristic information point. Open all year. ♦$$♦

a. Avenida Carlos Alessandri 1379, Algarrobo
t. +56 9 7904 5615
i. koruquiosco

Founded by a surfing couple, **La Surferia (64)** serves delicious tacos. While on any corner in Chile's cities and towns you'll find empanadas, fish and other typical Chilean food, La Surferia is Algarrobo's first taco place, spicing up your local menu with some Mexican tastes, cruelty free! Find them next to Algarrobo Restaurant and close to Cancha de Patinaje, the skate park. Open all year. ♦$$♦

a. Avenida Carlos Alessandri 1497 Local C, Algarrobo

Café Ferrieri Coffee (65) sits at Las Cruses viewpoint Punta del Lacho. Pretty perfect location for your morning cuppa! Open all year, opening times vary depending on season. ♦$♦

a. Mirador Punta del Lacho, Las Cruces, El Tabo
i. ferrieri_coffee

Santa Domingo doesn't have a great choice of beach restaurants, but having **Santa Pizza (66)** at the spot, you won't miss out. Santa Pizza is run by a surf, yoga and beach loving family, who've created a lovely place with a great vibe. Backed by dunes, they're right at the beach - the sea close enough to touch. Besides Italian food they've cocktails and wines on offer, and a collection of wines for sale too. Yoga classes are on the menu, on request. Open all year. ♦$$♦

a. Paseo del Mar 140, Santo Domingo
t. +56 9 8818 5585
i. santapizzacl

SHOP

Find gallery and book shop **Costa Central Chile** (**67**) in the same wooden premises as Santa Pizza. Their main focus is on the flora and fauna of Chile. The books, illustrations, postcards and accessories all relate to the local natural environment, and they're well stocked for such a small shop. Open every weekend and during holidays. ◆$$◆

a. Paseo del Mar 200, Santo Domingo
t. +56 9 5718 9427
w. costa-central-chile.ueniweb.com

SLEEP

La Tribu Ecolodge & Camping (**68**) is a delight. Resembling camping on the beach, what with their white sand grounds, but with all the blissful comforts like a 2-person sauna and hot tub, a yoga dome and swimming pool. It's a small-scale site with pitches for tents and vans, and cabanas for rent. Regular yoga retreats and workshops are on offer. Open all year. ◆$$◆

a. Camino Las Dichas Km 2, Algarrobo
t. +56 9 9476 6998
i. latribu_ecolodge

A few minutes' drive from several surf breaks in the area, find **Hostal La Tabla** (**69**). This cool, colorful and budget friendly place is pretty unique in that it has its own climbing wall, a gym and - how convenient! - a surf shop on the premises. Needless to say, as a guest, you have access to all. Ask your friendly host Chapu to help you plan your week in the area, and he'll probably throw in a couple of tips on the surf as well. Open all year. ◆$◆

a. Avenida La Montaña 0721, El Quisco
t. +56 9 9698 3240
i. hostallatabla

Camping El Bosque (**70**) is a large campsite at Playa la Castilla in El Tabo, with shaded pitches between the pine trees. Although basic, it's very child friendly; fun sculptures are spread along the site, you might set up your tent or van next to a giant dinosaur, or enjoy your lunch in a boat. It's a good option to stay if you want to visit some of the poets' houses and museums. Closed in winter. ◆$◆

a. Playa la Castilla, Avenida Baquedano, El Tabo
t. +56 9 7324 8133
fb. campingelbosqueeltabo

IN AND AROUND MATANZAS AND PUERTECILLO

◆

Although the waves and wind were always there, settlements like Matanzas and Puertecillo didn't start their gradual transformation into lively, hip and buzzing surfy towns until this century, really. Less than 3 hours (160 kms) away from Santiago, over the last couple of decades or so they've become a hub for wind, kite and surfers but all the while, still keeping their small fishing village vibes.

Matanzas offers a good choice of restaurants and pretty cool stays. Its harbor and gray sand beach, now frequented with ocean and watersports lovers, were once the stage for battles between the Spanish fleets and pirates, and sea lions were hunted for their 'blubber' (used for oil), meat and skin. Fortunately, today the marine mammals are left to do their thing; like fish, bark and hang out with their posse on Isla Pupuya. They share the small island just off the coast from Matanzas with pelicans and other seabirds.
Only a stone's throw away, and part of the Matanzas area, is La Vega de Pupuya, the tiniest of towns, which attracts bird watchers as much as it does surfers (with or without sail or kite).

Further south lies Puertecillo - a magical place if you ask us. Driving down the road into town, you'll see endless lines rolling into the southern end of the beach; an exposed, long left pointbreak with very consistent surf. From the late 1980s, surfers started visiting and camping out basic-style, but only if they had a 4 wheel drive to access the beach via the notoriously dangerous road, La Cuchilla - meaning 'The Knife', which seems a fitting name, in our opinion!

These days, the roads are a lot safer (one leading up to a high-end private condo) and so you'll find a different vibe at the end of them. You can understand why recent urban development is a somewhat controversial subject among the local community. You'll spot houses that look like dreams, and there's better infrastructure (road signs! Yay!) but part of the rough and ready hippy atmosphere's slowly wearing off too.

During the cooler hours of a summer's day, after your umpteenth surf session, you'll see families gathering at the beach or enjoying a sunset cocktail at the bar while kids play at the skateboard ramp. The sounds of rolling waves, birds chattering, children running around and people laughing linger in the air till well past sunset. A great place to keep you in the present moment and relax; for sure you won't hear a lot of traffic, and you might not have phone reception either.

TO DO

♦

We dare say, **Mirador de San Pedro** (**71**) to the north of Matanzas takes the word 'viewpoint' to the next level. Especially when you drive up here from the city with no idea what to expect. You're likely to be just as gobsmacked as we were by the impressive views over La Boca (the mouth), where the Rapel River meets the sea, the green hills and cliffs to the far north. The viewpoint's named after San Pedro, the protector of fishermen, his statue looking out over the estuary.

a. Mirador de San Pedro, Navidad

Wind being one of the main attractions of the Matanzas (and in particular

La Vega de Pupuya) area, you can expect to feel like you've arrived in the kitesurfers' promised land. Want to join the fun? **SideOn** (**72**) offer kite lessons with all equipment provided and plenty of other outdoor experiences too, such as kayaking and SUP expeditions, or in winter freeski and snowkite in the Andes mountains. Instructors are certified and knowledgeable, and lessons are available in English. Open all year.

a. Costanera de Matanzas
t. +56 9 9905 3148
i. sideonchile

Roll out your mat in Hotel Surazo's yoga shala and get stretchy. The space also serves as a communal living room for hotel guests and has a

fireplace for you to get you warm, cozy and potentially sweaty. **Yoga classes** (**73**) are included if you're staying at the hotel (so there are zero valid excuses not to join as it's a maximum 20 steps from your bed!) and open to non-residents too - book at the reception. Open all year.

a. Carlos Ibáñez del Campo, Matanzas
t. +56 9 9600 0110
w. surazo.cl
i. hotelsurazo

Parque Reserva El Maitén (**74**) is a privately-owned nature reserve, conservation and community project, in which native flora and forests are protected, while a community of nature and outdoor sports lovers can hike, mountain bike or wander in a daydreamy state and enjoy the beauty. The owners have dedicated 100 hectares of land to create an outdoor sports park, with a large variety of trekking trails, playground, pump track and about 15 MTB circuits - routes for all levels, from family-friendly to hardcore trails. During the creation of the Parque, old local settlements were discovered which revealed some of the history behind the valley - you can see artifacts and learn more about them at the Museo del Campo Maitén. Open all year.

- **a.** Reserva El Maitén, along the G-866, Navidad
- **t.** +56 9 3884 9722
- **w.** reservaelmaiten.cl

From the southern end of Puertecillo beach, you can walk through the forest and along the cliffs for a spectacular view of the entire beach and the surf. The nature trail **Sendero de la Naturaleza** (**75**) leads you along a narrow path and down to the next beach, Punta Santo Domingo (not to be confused with Santo Domingo beach in Valparaíso), where the locals collect Cochayuyo - a popular algae/seaweed used as a classic ingredient in Chilean cuisine for thousands of years. If you're lucky you might see some penguins on the rocks too!

- **a.** Puertecillo Beach

EAT/DRINK/HANG OUT
◆

One of our favorite dining options is the restaurant at **Hotel Surazo** (**76**), run by a dedicated chef who acquired his fine skills in France. His love for the wind and waves led him back to Chile and straight to Matanzas, where he and his friends set up this contemporary restaurant and hotel

right by the beach. The place is built around a number of trees, which create - along with window-walls and smart lighting - a striking style of architecture that feels outside-inside in the best way. If that's still too indoorsy for you, you can choose to sit on the beach terrace, next to the firepit. On the menu, lots of veggie options alongside local meat and seafood, each dish with surprising and inspiring ingredients, creating a delicious fusion of high-quality Chilean ingredients and French techniques (très bon!). It's safe to say that if the place itself doesn't make your heart and soul sing, the food will. Open all year for lunch, dinner, and drinks. ◆$$$◆

- **a.** Carlos Ibáñez del Campo, Matanzas
- **t.** +56 9 9600 0110
- **w.** surazo.cl

One of the best pizzas we had in Chile (and we had many) must be at **Pizzeria Matanzas** (**77**), run by the lovely Sofi. The veggie menu's longer than your surfboard, with vegan options aplenty. The pizzeria started a few years ago as a pop-up food truck and has grown in popularity, and therefore in size, little by little, until it became today's cozy restaurant with outdoor terrace. Don't hesitate to say hi to Sofi's four-legged friend; he'll be happy to cuddle up and very keen to help out if you have any leftovers. Open all year. ◆$$◆

- **a.** Camino Lagunillas, Matanzas
- **t.** +56 9 8881 3859
- **i.** lapizzeriamatanzas

Ruda Coffee (**78**) is a cute coffee place on the boulevard Matanzas Costanera, where you're welcome to bring your laptop and (try to) do some work while swigging a kombucha, or one of the many cafecito variations. They've tasty snacks to tempt you to stay longer too, from sourdough sandwiches, empanadas and tostadas to slices of sweetness - oooh the droolworthy cakes! Wifi (good and fast) is free to make use of while you sup or snack. Open all year. ◆$◆

- **a.** La Costanera, Matanzas
- **i.** ruda.matanzas

Whether you want to grab lunch with your kids, have a romantic sunset cocktail with your better half, or meet a bunch of fun, ocean-loving locals on a night out at the weekend, **La Lobera** (**79**) bar and restaurant at Playa Pupuya is your place. During the week, lots of locals drop in to hang out with

their neighbors while the dogs and kids have a playdate in the sand. This is the place to be on a Friday night, when the tables are put aside and the DJ starts playing. The absolute best location to watch the kiters, and you can make use of their storage and changing rooms, and inflate your kite. Open all year. ◆$$$◆

a. Playa Pupuya, Vega de la Pupuya
t. +56 9 9597 1613
w. laloberaclub.cl

The mix of wood and floor-to-ceiling windows overlooking Pupuya beach make restaurant **Márola (80)** a mighty fine and fancy choice to go for cocktails at their beautiful bar. If your budget allows, you'll probably want to stick around for dinner too. If you

prefer to go all the way - triple fancy - you can book to stay in one of their sturdy-looking cabins, with views over the beach or the wetlands. Open all year. ◆$$$◆

a. Pupuya Beach, Vega de la Pupuya
t. +56 9 6636 1894
w. marola.cl

Literally on the beach of Puertecillo, within walking distance of the surf break, you'll find **Taranguita Puertecillo (81)**. Great for lunch, dinner, sunset drinks or to fuel up with a snack between surf sessions. The owners want to make sure you can taste the 'flavors of the land' in their dishes. Sit down and relax, while spotting Santiaguinos freshly arrived from the city to spend the weekend in their wooden beach houses. Open all year. ◆$$$◆

a. Punta Puertecillo
t. +56 9 4117 2040
fb. Taringuita Puertecillo

After a long day of fun stuff, when all you want is to rinse off the salt and sand and eat, eat, eat, family-run La **Estacion Pizzeria (82)** is your new best friend. Even the hungriest of the hungry don't need to order more than one pizza - one will fill up two of you, for sure. The place is relaxed and rustic, very child and pet friendly, they've vegan options too, and you can eat your pizza around a huge open fireplace discussing tomorrow's forecast with your neighbors, or grab a cozy table for two. Great atmosphere and friendly vibes all over! Find them in Tumán, a hamlet just east of Puertecillo. Open all year, opening hours vary but usually open weekends only, after 18:00. ♦$$♦

a. G-880 470, Tumán
t. +56 9 8424 7740
fb. La Estación Pizzeria y Almacen

Another good pizza option in Puerte is **Torino's Pizza** (83), located on the northern side of the village directly in front of the beach. You'll be served tasty stone-baked pizzas and cold craft beers by the owners themselves. What a combo! Open all year. ♦$$♦

a. Bajada Peatonal a Puertecilla, Playa Puertecillo
i. torinos.pizza

Driving inland from Puertecillo to your next destination, there's a good chance you'll pass the little town of Litueche; a handy stop-off to fuel up and/or get camping supplies. If so, do stop by **Tía Yoli** (84) restaurant while you're in town. No hip no happening here but big-time popular among the surf community, as you can tell from her famous wall of stickers - spot ours! Tía Yoli will give you a taste of the real home-made food that Chileans are served by their favorite tía (aunt) or grandma. Prepared with love to make happy heart and belly, with big side portions and all at a very affordable price. And a little advice from experience: don't eat too much bread with 'Pebre' (Chilean sauce) or you'll be full before you've begun. Open all year. ♦$♦

a. Hermanos Carrera 650, Litueche
t. +56 9 8970 5433
fb. Hosteria Yoli Litueche

SHOP
♦

Run by artsy local Claudia, **Arte Mandala** (85) is a little store packed with healthy goodness and all things natural. From refills of grains, nuts, seeds and staple cupboard essentials to organic teas, bio beauty products, sun care creams and local deli goodies. If you support a sustainable lifestyle, we promise this place will make your heart beat happier. Claudia has two stores in Matanzas. Open all year.

a. Calle Principal de Matanzas (Casa Roca) / Costanera de Matanzas (Store 3)
i. artemandalamatanzas

SLEEP
♦

At the tip of La Boca, down a long bumpy dirt road on top of a cliff, you'll find the unforgettably magical **Los Cisnes** (86). This beautiful spot is as peaceful as can be - the only noise around being bird calls and the rolling

sound of the Rapel River meeting the ocean - with options of staying on the basic (and very gentle on your budget) campsite or hopping up a few notches and treating yourself to a stay in one of the wooden cabanas (sleeping up to 8 persons). You can also book lessons for kayak, SUP, wind or kite surf at the on-site Centro Náutico, where regular events and competitions are held. Whatever you choose, you'll receive a warm friendly welcome from Nibaldo Maturana, the sexta-maybe-septuagenarian bonafide seaside explorer who has many fine adventure stories to share. Open all year. ♦$♦

a. Desembocadura Rio Rapel, Parcela 52A, La Boca
t. +56 9 9139 5939
w. loscisnes.cl

Already mentioned in the Eat section, **Hotel Surazo** (87) is possibly one of our favorite hotels in central Chile. Pure and simple, while classy and exquisite at the same time. Nature is right at the heart of their tv-free, spacious rooms that all have their own private wooden deck. The outstanding style is partly down to its architecture - built around ancient trees that continue to grow through the building designed around them. You've a bar

and restaurant on the side, and whether you opt to roll out your yoga mat - classes included with your stay - step into the hot tub, or sit back and relax with a glass of wine, you'll have the beautiful backdrop of nature, the beach, and at night a clear starry sky. Open all year. ◆$$$◆

a. Carlos Ibáñez del Campo, Matanzas
t. +56 9 9600 0110
w. surazo.cl

Located in the middle of a pine forest, only 150 meters from the beach, **Camping OMZ (88)** is a great choice if you're traveling in your campervan and/or with children - charges are per pitch so if you're traveling solo it's unlikely to be your cheapest option. They've BBQ areas, a big 'Quincho' (common area) and facilities to wash your dishes, and each site has its own private bathroom - total luxury, considering the usual very basic Chilean bathroom standards! If camping's not your style, or you've a mind to splash-out and treat yourself, they've spacious wooden cabins for rent too. Enjoy the connection with nature, the meditative sound of waves breaking on rocks in the distance, and, undoubtedly, some really good quality peaceful sleep! Open all year. ◆$$◆

a. Fundo San Luis Lagunillas, Matanzas
t. +56 9 9643 4809
w. omz.cl

Find another camping option, with basic facilities but a great vibe, at **Camping Playa de Matanzas (89)**, right at the playa. Surrounded by pine forest, you can park your van or set up your tent, and if you're lucky, grab a spot close to the campfires. We say basic as in rustic; outdoor wooden stalls with individual toilets and warm showers, but you've all the mod-cons like a washing up area, picnic tables and wifi too! If you bring your pet, he or she will be wise to take you for a beach walk at sunrise. Ah, the beauty of it! Open all year. ◆$◆

a. Fundo San Luis Lagunillas, Matanzas
t. +56 9 4152 3513
w. playadematanzas.cl

Think twice before booking **Quadro (90)** if you're afraid of heights! If not, this is the definition of freedom.

Perched on top of a cliff just outside town, these smart-looking wooden and glass cabanas sleep up to 6 people (2 bedrooms, 2 bathrooms, and a sofa-bed). Both bedrooms are located on the top floor, so you'll likely wake up and imagine for a moment that you're flying over the coast. The deck comes with a windshield, to shelter you from wind while lounging in your private hot tub or using the outdoor BBQ. If you drive from Matanzas to Pupuya on the Ruta G-890 (or the other way round), you'll need to turn towards the beach and look for the big wooden gate - open it and drive through to the spectastical view! Open all year. ◆$$◆

a. Pupuya, Matanzas
t. +56 9 8475 6735
w. quadromatanzas.com

Simple y Puro (**91**) offer 4 rather classy 2-person apartments with high-end facilities, like heating, rain shower, and hot tub with bubble function overlooking the ocean. If that doesn't help you fully relax and recover after an active day, we don't know what will! If you're looking for comfort and style, you've made a good choice here. Located at the northern coastal side of Pupuya, next to Pupuya Beach and La Lobera Club. Open all year. ◆$$$◆

a. Pupuya, Matanzas
t. +56 9 3912 5688
w. simpleypuro.com

The apartments of **25 Nudos Lodge** (**92**) will give you the comfort and rest you need after an intense time of traveling or exploring the neighborhood. Each apartment's equipped to sleep up to 4 people and has a private terrace where you have a grill, hot tub and, of course, an amazing ocean view. And the place is dog friendly too. Find them at the end of the same dirt road as Simple y Puro - keep going until you see it on your right. Open all year. ◆$$$◆

a. Pupuya, Matanzas
t. +56 9 8728 8235
w. 25nudoslodge.com

Following Camino Puertecillo heading north, only minutes away from a perfect world class surf break, **Puertezion** (**93**) is one of those places that's hard to capture in words. It's a surf hostel and surf school in one, but the fairytale vibe and dreamy garden almost make you forget about the ocean for a while. Almost, of course… Puertezion is a great site to bring your kids, and a magical place to watch the sun set. At night, you can sit at the communal fireplace, surrounded by big old trees, gaze up at the stars and listen to the ocean's soundtrack, while you sizzle your dinner on the grill. Run by surfer couple Manu & Titan, who

met at this very place and decided to build their hostel, back in the day. Their passion for the lifestyle, surf and nature is embodied in this unique accommodation. Choose a private loft, an apartment to bring your little ones/friends, or if you're backpacking and budgeting, throw your bag on one of the bunk beds. Open all year. ◆$$◆

a. Puertecillo, Litueche
w. puertezion.com

At the end of the road, when you almost can't drive any further, at the northern edge of the village, find **Puertecillo Norte Camping** (**94**). The friendly owner used to be a surfer himself, you can ask him any questions and he'll be happy to help. The camping's quite basic but has everything you need, including a warm shower. The terrain has an interesting layout, with terraced pitches, so *top tip* (flashing the cheerleader pom-poms at ya) choose one higher up for an ocean view. Open all year. ◆$◆

a. Bajasa Peatonal a Puertecillo, Puertecillo, Litueche
t. +56 9 9667 9630
i. puertecillonorte

Photo: Maikel Kersbergen

BACKBEND: URDHVA MUKHA SVANASANA

Upward Facing Dog

This pose will help your pop ups feel more fluid and also relieves tension; it feels great before and after a big paddle-out.

Strength and mobility are equally important when it comes to surfing. Incorporating a backbend like upward facing dog in your warm-up routine helps to lengthen and strengthen the spine and increase your range of motion.

Benefits:
Improves mobility of the spine, strengthens the back and glutes, opens the chest and shoulders. Can help to prevent shoulder or back injuries caused by repetitive movements.

How:
Lie on your front, legs stretched out behind you, and place your hands palms down under the shoulders. Push the tops of your feet down, squeeze your glutes to protect your lower back, then roll your shoulders back, moving slightly forward while lifting your chest up, keeping a slight bend in your arms and your ears away from your shoulders. If you're comfortable here, you can also lift hips and knees off the ground. Try to avoid sinking your hips down. For optimal spine mobility, practice dynamically by adding a counter movement: go from upward dog to child's pose - move to a kneeling position, buttocks on feet, chest to your thighs, arms forward, face down - and repeat.

IN AND AROUND PICHILEMU

•

As an ocean-loving explorer, a visit to surf town Pichilemu - the declared heritage town surrounded by lagoons and forest - is surely on your tick list. If not, then most likely the famous point break just outside of town, Punta de Lobos, is in its place. This point's a dedicated World Surfing Reserve, the celeb amongst big wave surf spots, where famed competitions are held each year, like the Quiksilver Ceremonial Punta de Lobos Big Wave Invitational. Si, si, that's quite a mouthful - you can probably get away with calling it the Quiksilver Ceremonial while you're in the neighborhood! And if the name Ramón Navarro doesn't ring a bell, maybe read a bit about him and his work on the conservation of the point in our Save the Waves write-up before you visit his hometown; just in case you have the honor of sharing a bit of sea or, in fact, any space with him.

In the last two decades or so, Pichilemu town - its name derived from the native Mapudungun language, little (pichi) forest (lemu) - has grown from a seaside resort into a hub for national and international folks who choose to live near the ocean, with epic conditions for all sorts of watersports on their doorstep. Add the constant flow of surf tourists and, being so close to Santiago, the city people escaping, well… the city for the weekend, boards strapped to the roof of their cars, it's lively for sure.

While Pichilemu is a buzzing town, Punta de Lobos is quieter and (not yet) too urbanized. It has a slightly more alternative and surfier vibe. As a result of the growth in the last years, both towns have an impressive choice of restaurants and guesthouses, from unassuming to organic, from basic to luxurious. But the heart of Pichilemu with its low-rise family houses and dusty roads, gray sand beaches and hilly surroundings, remains the same; celebrating an outdoorsy lifestyle where everything seems to revolve around the waves. Though, having said that, there are plenty fun things to do besides surfing.

TO DO

◆

On the very rare occasion that the ocean's flat - a practically non-existent problem in Punta de Lobos - you've the terra firma option to grab your skateboard or join a skateboard class at **Hotel Alaia's Skate Park (95)**. The 'concrete' is in fact made from cut black rock, upcycled and reused after the 2010 earthquake. The skate park's ideal for children and adults alike, to learn, improve or just have some playtime, and is a safe, relaxed hangout for skate, BMX, rollers and inline skates. Right next to the park is a **bouldering wall (96)** for those wanting to limber up their hands (and legs) with some climbing practice. And the best perk - both the wall and bowl overlook Punta de Lobos beach. Open all year (to non-residents too).

a. Camino Punta de Lobos 681, Pichilemu
t. +56 9 5701 5971
w. hotelalaia.com

A little detour inland from Punta de Lobos sits local craft beer **brewery Viejo Lobo (97)**. Founder Arnaud Frennet is a big wave windsurfer from Belgium, who moved here to live near the ocean. Easy to guess why he chose Punta de Lobos to create his great beers, eh? Inspired by the traditions of his Belgian beer-brewing uncle - who happened to be an influential monk at the Abbaye Notre-Dame d'Orval, well known for its production of the Trappist beer Orval

- and with the help of friends, Arnaud spent over ten years brewing, tasting and perfecting his recipe. And that's how the Viejo Lobo beer was born; fermented a few steps from the sea and matured in a cellar under the sand, all combining to put the 'special' in this specialty beer. His passion and craftsmanship show in the details, like labeling all bottles uniquely, showing the week the beer was bottled. Open all year, reservations required, and if you go, please say hi from us.

a. Camino interior Punta de Lobos, Pichilemu
t. +56 9 7494 9405
w. viejolobo.cl

It's not always easy to keep the mind and body connected and flexible while

on the road. Taking a yoga class is, therefore, always a bright idea - a bit of meditation, stretching and movement while listening to the mantras of the waves. When the weather allows, **yoga classes at Hotel Alaia (98)** are held outside, adding some extra seaside ointment to your practice. All levels, non-residents and drops-ins are welcome too. Open all year.

a. Camino Punta de Lobos 681, Pichilemu
t. +56 9 5701 5971
w. hotelalaia.com

Even if big wave surfing's well out of your league, as it is for most of us mortal beings, it's still well worth the drive to Punta de Lobos to watch the surfers from the **viewpoint of Los Morros (99)** at the end of the cliff. As you walk out along the path, take a minute to appreciate your surroundings. This area was saved from development by the community-led Fundación Punta de Lobos to conserve the biodiversity and landscape and preserve public access - find more information on the signs you'll pass by. And don't forget your camera! Though be prepared to share the space with fellow spectators, who no doubt want a shot of this iconic spot too.

a. Punta de Lobos, Pichilemu

At **Salinas de Cáhuil (100)** just north of Punta de Lobos, time appears to have stood still. You might see Huasos (Chilean cowboys) wearing traditional clothing riding along on their horses, and at the Salinas, the local 'salineros' continue to harvest salt using techniques that have been passed down for hundreds of years. You can take a tour of the saltworks - considered Tesoro Humano Vivo (Living Human Treasure) by UNESCO - to learn about the craft and production process and, depending on the time of year, may get to see the surreally reddish-pink water, a result of the process. The salt's apparently healthier than most iodized salts due to lower levels of sodium, so why not give it a try and support the local community by buying some during your visit. Open all year.

a. Along the I-520, 2 kms south of Cáhuil

If you want to add a little variety to your paddling routine after woahh-so-much-surf-time (or skip the surf time entirely in favor of a more peaceful experience) why not opt for a SUP or kayak tour in the **Lagoon of Cáhuil (101)**. The surrounding wetlands make it very tranquilo in comparison to the coast and the perfect place to do a spot of birdwatching - perhaps see black-necked swans, which are native to the southern areas of South America. The lagoon's easy to find; you can't miss it as you drive from Punta de Lobos towards Cáhuil town. SUP and kayak rentals are available at several stalls along the river.

a. Cáhuil

Here's your opportunity to discover some about the world-famous wine region and explore the Colchagua Valley and Santa Cruz. Somewhat inland but then again, inland's never too far from the coast and you're sure to enjoy the scenery on the drive. As one of the most important areas for wine production in Chile, there are several wineries in the valley that offer wine tasting. **Colchagua Wine Tours (102)** offer day tours, which include pick up and drop back to nearby locations in Santa Cruz, so you can get into the tasting without any driving worries! From deluxe tours with lunch included, to custom-tailored with optional add-ons like nature walks, trekking, make your own wine, and cooking classes. Open all year.

a. Colchagua
t. +56 9 8936 1161
w. colchaguawinetours.com

While you're exploring a bit of inland territory, gain some insight into Chile's history and cultural heritage by visiting the **Colchagua Museum (103)** in Santa Cruz. The museum, set in a typical colonial house, displays objects and artifacts from as far back as the beginning of life and the Inca empire up until the present day. Open all year.

a. Avenida Presidente Errázuriz 145, Santa Cruz
t. +56 72 282 1050
w. museocolchagua.cl

EAT/DRINK/HANG OUT
◆

Pulpo (104) is perhaps the only place along Chile's 4000 km coastline that makes you feel like you're in a funky European city, instead of South America. A mural of a huge purple octopus (pulpo) covers the wall of the backyard, while inside the walls are adorned with graffiti, plants, art and surfboards. Owner Chris opened Pulpo in 2014, having picked the name based on the title of the worst song the Beatles ever made (his words). You can walk in any time on any given day and find a great atmosphere here. On the menu, you'll find an interesting mix from ceviche to (really good!) pizzas, from fancy cocktails to cheap beers, and at the weekend, you'll find a DJ creating a lively urban vibe. No wonder this place is popular with locals, tourists and families alike. Definitely the place to be if you're in the mood for some party vibes. We heard the mojito and pisco sour they serve are famous all around town. Gosh, they're even pet friendly! Go, snoop dog. Open all year, every day, every night. ◆$$◆

a. Daniel Ortúzar 275, Pichilemu
t. +56 9 5456 4160
i. pulpo_bar_pizzeria_

Sanguchería La Casa Verde (105) is, pretty obviously, located in a green-colored house, but their food and mindset are also pretty green. All the furniture is made from reclaimed and recycled wood, it's pet-friendly, and the menu (filled with more than just sandwiches!) will meet the approval of both vegan and meat-loving foodies. Add an ocean view, generous portions, great cocktails and fresh juices and it's no wonder that it's always busy here. Open all year. ◆$$◆

a. Daniel Ortúzar 215, Pichilemu
t. +56 9 2093 6331
w. lacasaverde.cl

Finding quality Asian food on the Chilean coast is a quite a feat. If you're a big fan, like us, and it's as good as restaurant **Cúrcuma (106)** serves it, you'll want to come back for breakfast, lunch and dinner. Every day! Chilean/Indian owner Nihal has the most friendly, welcoming energy. He knows how to make food that comforts your belly, heart and soul - food that's fresh, healthy and 100% made from scratch (they even grow their own chai spices). The menu has a grand selection of vegetarian and vegan dishes, since that's what Nihal was looking for but couldn't find when he first moved to town. You can drop into this well-known hotspot any time of the day: think home-baked bread or an acai bowl in the morning, a coffee or smoothie (ask for an extra maca or spirulina shot) while logging in for some remote work, a delicious pad thai at lunch, homemade ice cream on a hot afternoon, and heartwarming Indian curry at night. Despite the success of Cúrcuma, Nihal's not considering opening a second location - 'Why grow if you can enjoy what you already have?' he says. We can't argue with that. Open all year. ♦$$♦

a. Avenida Comercio 224, Pichilemu
t. +56 9 9509 0670
i. curcuma_pichilemu

Heladería Buena Mano (107) is a small, minimalistic place, serving delicious ice creams in funky flavor combinations such as Lemon Basil and Coco Banana. This tiny place is packed with goodness so expect long queues in summer - but they're worth the wait. Options include a good selection of vegan, sugar-free and lactose-free, making this a good joint for guilt-free ice cream. Open all year, from Thursday to Monday. (Usually closed for a few weeks in winter for a well-deserved holiday). ♦$$♦

a. Avenida Comercio 1926, Pichilemu
t. +56 9 8620 3042
i. buenamanohelados

Cute little bakery and coffee stop **Planta (108)** not only uses lots of plants in their décor, absolutely everything on the menu is plant-based too. Enjoy a coffee in the sun on the terrace, and in case you get hungry but can't decide between the choices on offer; we highly recommend their empanadas! Plenty of gluten-free options too. Open all year (closed on Mondays). ♦$$♦

a. Avenida Comercio 2241 Local 2, Pichilemu
t. +56 9 3190 5085
i. planta_pichilemu

Eating at **Hotel Alaia (109)** is fine dining at its best. Most ingredients are from their own huerto, fresh off the land and onto your plate - always seasonal and as local as it gets. Instead of building more rooms, the hotel dedicated a large piece of their land to creating a vegetable garden and orchard, thus staying true to their vision on low-impact and sustainable hospitality. You can even visit the huerto and learn about their holistic, organic, earth-friendly approach to agriculture - not using any fertilizers or pesticides. The combination of the luxurious and spacious restaurant with its huge windows and big fireplace creates a warm atmosphere, all dishes are dressed beautifully, and the staff are ever so attentive. Open all year, reservations required. ♦$$$$♦

a. Camino Punta de Lobos 681, Pichilemu
t. +56 9 5701 5971
w. hotelalaia.com

Unassuming-looking restaurant and hostel **Club Si Ma (110)** is frequented by locals and offers homemade Chilean food at a very affordable price. Before entering you can check the daily menu on a blackboard. If you like what you see, sit either inside or in their courtyard. Open all year. ♦$♦ ♦$$♦

a. Carrera 319 / Dionisio Acevedo 324, Pichilemu
t. +56 9 7550 1521
i. sima_pichilemu

'We are not a bar, we are not a restaurant, we are a Social Club', explains one of the initiators of **Los Piures, Club Social (111)**. Set up in an old warehouse, Los Piures is a place to enjoy good seasonal food and ocean culture, serving as a meeting

point for everyone who enjoys both. Furthermore, craft beers and cocktails, regular live music, films and all sort of events and workshops are on offer, there's a community garden and a play area for kids. Perfect place to mingle, we'd say. Open all year. ◆$◆ ◆$$◆

a. Camino Punta de Lobos Lote 3.3, Pichilemu
t. +56 9 2259 3204
w. landing.lospiures.cl

Sit on the small terrace of **Punta De Choclo (112)** overlooking Punta Lobos beach, keeping one eye on the waves while trying to choose whether to go for their quinoa or açai bowl, a hot chocolate or a freshly squeezed juice. The kiosk is located right in front of the wooden stairs down to the beach. Open all year during weekends and holidays.

a. Punta de Lobos, Pichilemu
t. +56 9 9239 6797
i. puntadechoclo

Walking along the path that leads to the restaurant of **Cuarzo Lodge (113)**, you'll pass buzzing bees checking out every flower, a natural pool surrounded by plants, and quartz stones glinting in the sun. Built on top of their yoga room, the restaurant extends onto a rooftop terrace with a view of the waves of Punta de Lobos in the distance. Food is great, tasty and wholesome, with plenty of plant-based options. Stop for lunch or a romantic sunset dinner at this classy but welcoming restaurant. Open all year. ◆$$$◆

a. Punta de Lobos, Pichilemu
t. +56 9 4245 2202
w. cuarzolodge.cl

If you're in or around Cáhuil, we recommend a stop at **Marea Baja Cafe Pizzería (114)**. Great pizzas, good vibes and a large terrace to hang out. They're also proof that beautiful, traditional Cáhuil isn't lagging behind modern times - with vegan options available! Open all year from Wednesday to Sunday. ◆$$◆

a. Camino Público de Cáhuil 1997, Cáhuil
t. +56 9 4808 8514
i. mareabajacahuil

SHOP

Local souvenirs on offer at **Boldo Aires Chilenos** (**115**) range from clothes, bags, trinkets, ceramics and jewelry to edibles and beauty products, the majority of which are handmade locally, sustainable and 100% made 'con amor'. Open all year.

a. Avenida Comercio 2621, Pichilemu
i. boldoaireschilenospichilemu

Plans to buy a beach house in Pichilemu? You may well be tempted! Or want to take the ocean vibe home with you? Get inspired by everything you see in **Eva Artesanía y Decoración** (**116**). Various styles, from super colorful to classy classic, make it hard to leave without buying something, anything, everything really. Open all year.

a. Avenida Comercio 2241 Local 04, Pichilemu
t. +56 9 5618 6264
i. evapichilemu

Wild Lama (**117**) could be one of the coolest outdoor clothing stores in the area, and we're not just talking about the stylish outfits. They've an inspiring vision, focusing on organic materials,

recycling, reusing, and making clothes ethically while giving back to local communities. And to put their money where their mouth is, they work closely with local non-profit organizations who protect Chile's nature areas. Open all year.

a. Avenida Comercio 2241 Local 12, Pichilemu
t. +56 9 3933 9868
w. wildlama.com

If the Asian vibes at restaurant Cúrcuma are your cup of chai, **Aarati** (**118**) is the place to wander around next. Maybe with your belly still full, digesting your food while immersing yourself in all that's Eastern. All clothes, accessories and interior decorations are created in India or Bali, adding beautiful bright colors, prints and a refreshing change from your daily black wetsuit-wear. Open all year.

a. Avenida Comercio 2241 Local 22, Pichilemu
t. +56 9 9509 0670

By now you may have noticed that precise address info in Chile can be somewhat, err… loose, to say the least. Same goes for café and health store **Almacén conSiente** (**119**). Just

look for the wooden sign of a big blue eye located about 300 meters before the intersection of Punta de Lobos. Easy that one! Besides treats such as cinnamon buns, you can stock up on or refill your beans, nuts, dried fruits, oats, rice and much more. Open all year.

a. Punta de Lobos, Pichilemu
i. almacenconsiente

SLEEP

Between surf breaks La Puntilla and Infiernillo find **Eco Camping La Caletilla** (**120**), a basic camp site with very affordable prices. They've pitches for tents and (small) campervans, and all pitches have a little shack made from reclaimed wood for some shade and wind protection, a BBQ and picnic table. Services include warm showers, electricity, and friendly staff. There's a playground for toddlers and grocery stores are nearby. Open all year.
◆$◆ ◆$$◆

a. Eugenio Suárez 905, Pichilemu
t. +56 9 9216 7640
w. campinglacaletilla.cl

Check the waves from your tent or campervan at **Camping La Puntilla**

(**121**), located in front of the beach. (Mostly) shaded pitches with a priceless view, warm showers, basic and budget friendly. Open all year. ♦$♦ ♦$$♦

a. Eugenio Díaz Lira 5, Pichilemu (access from Avenida Costanera)
t. +56 9 6589 8677
w. camping.puntilla.cl

Check the surf from your bed at **Casas Costa Luna** (**122**), and maybe spot a squadron of pelicans flying

by too. Their wooden guesthouses, named after the children of the lovely (English-speaking) owner Carolina, are comfy, equipped with a kitchenette and terrace and just steps away from the ocean. The larger house is built in a diamond shape and has windows all around, giving you an almost 360-degree view - yoooowweeee! You can sense Carolina's love for details in the use of reclaimed and upcycled materials; our favorite is the old skool bathtub that serves as an outdoor shower to rinse off after a beach day. A sweet romantic option for couples but also great for groups or families - one house sleeps up to 4 people. Open all year. ♦$$$♦

a. Avenida Costanera 913, Pichilemu
t. +56 9 9779 0055
i. casas_costaluna

Still close to the beach but with a very different vibe, **Buda Lodge** (**123**) is set in Pichilemu's forest. They've a number of tiny houses and cabins in various sizes, styles and contemporary designs. A wooden path connects all houses, but it's designed in such a way you'll feel like you've got the forest all to yourself. Breakfast that's delivered to your door and a private hot tub are included. Open all year. ♦$$♦ ♦$$$♦

a. Evaristo Merino 1080, Pichilemu
t. +56 9 8190 3527
i. budalodge

Find **Lodge del Mar** (**124**) on an untouched piece of the coast between Pichilemu town and Punta de Lobos. This part of the coast is quiet even in high season, and the beach might feel

like a private one. On offer are modern and smartly designed hotel rooms for two, and spacious cabanas with private hot tubs on the decks, sleeping up to 6 guests. The set-up means all cabins and rooms face the huge garden, the sleek-looking outdoor pool, and the endless gray sand beach and ocean beyond. Open all year. ◆$$$◆

- **a.** Camino Cáhuil 3011, Playa Hermosa, Pichilemu
- **t.** +56 9 4220 9582
- **w.** lodgedelmar.cl

Aah… **Hotel Alaia** (**125**). We cherry-pick and love all our addresses equally, but some cherries sit on top of the cake of surf lodging. We've mentioned the hotel already, a couple of times, in the To Do and Eat sections, and obviously, we recommend a stay too (if budget allows). Hey, you might bump into a pro-surfer or two! Set in a unique location overlooking big wave spot Punta de Lobos, the owners have created a high-end, utterly tasteful and welcoming world where they combine exclusivity with low-impact hospitality. Alaia not only make a conscious effort to reduce their impact, but also work together with Fundación Punta de Lobos to protect the natural sanctuary of Punta de Lobos. The hotel has only 12 rooms on their large premises, keeping plenty of space for nature to thrive. The minimalist-design rooms are spacious, with all the conveniences you might need and just the right amount of luxurious comfort without extravagance. Open all year. ◆$$$$$◆

- **a.** Camino Punta de Lobos 681, Pichilemu
- **t.** +56 9 5701 5971
- **w.** hotelalaia.com

Less of a budget-burner but cool all the same is **Sirena Insolente Hostel** (**126**). Meet fellow travelers in the communal garden, balancing on the slackline or playing ping pong. Prepare your favorite meal together in the fully equipped kitchen and chill out and share paddling stories after hours spent in the surf, or other stories if you didn't do the surf thing… There are shared rooms as well as private rooms, and surf rentals are on offer too. Open all year. ◆$$◆

- **a.** Pasaje Punta de Lobos 169, Pichilemu
- **t.** +56 9 5856 5784
- **w.** sirenainsolentehostel.cl

Surf Lodge Punta de Lobos (127) is the brainchild of a Belgian windsurfer and artist (ask to see his beautiful drawings). The lodge is made from wood and located in the middle of the forest, and while it's a bit of a way from the beach, it more than makes up for that with its comfort and style. Choose a double, triple or shared room (sleeping 4), make yourself at home in the two-story communal living room, with floor to ceiling windows and swing chair, unwind in one of the 2 kick-ass swimming pools, or book the spa for a pamper night. Bike and board rentals can be arranged, as well as surfing and yoga classes. Open all year. ♦$$$♦

a. Catrianca, Lot B, Punta de Lobos, Pichilemu
t. +56 9 8154 1106
w. surflodgepuntadelobos.cl

In the upper part of Punta de Lobos, out of town and only a minute's drive from the beach, small-scale **Olas de Chile Ecocamp (128)** is a wonderful place to park up your van and set up camp for a few days. They've pitches for tents too - some shaded under elevated wooden terraces. And while you're here camping out, do enjoy their bathrooms, they're way above average compared to most Chilean camping standards. Open all year. ♦$$♦

a. Punta de Lobos, Pichilemu
t. +56 9 5450 4499
w. olasdechile.cl

If you're traveling with a tight budget and you're content with the simple things in life, **Camping Anton (129)** could well be just the place for you! A friendly American dude will make you feel welcome with his loud laughter, sharing a beer or 2, and will probably light the bonfire at night. This former pro snowboarder fell in love with Pichilemu on one of his snowboard trips to Chile and bought a piece of land to pursue his dream of living by the ocean. Although his main business is renting out his basic wooden cabins, he'll be happy to let you park up your campervan and use the bathroom for a few 'lucas' (1000 Chilean peso bills). Or, of course, opt for a cabin if you want a break from vanlife. Here's the treat; you won't find any info online, simply keep an eye out on the drive to Punta de Lobos till you see his sign, just before the turning right to Punta de Lobos beach. Then take a right and drive all the way through. Open all year. ♦$♦

a. Punta de Lobos, Pichilemu

SURF

◆

One of the most popular surf destinations in the country, Central Chile's appeal is not only consistent waves but also the simple fact of being close to the capital, easier and quicker to get to. Add a couple of coastal cities - Valparaíso and Viña del Mar - and a few holiday resorts, plus first-class pointbreaks, beachbreaks, small and big (BIG) wave options and you find a lot more people around than the other surf sections. Although crowds do thin in winter, the cold water (an sich) doesn't discourage many surfers. Even at the height of summer, in January and February, when air temperatures have you huffing and puffing, you'll want a 4.3 wetsuit, and booties are recommended most of the time.

While the Valparaíso region has quite a holiday vibe in summer, it's not all that surfy. The seaside settlements along this coast are favorite escapes for city-dwellers from Santiago and the area's fairly urbanized. One of the good things is that you can easily switch from surf to city break. Towns in the south of Central Chile - like Punta Lobos, Pichilemu, Puertecillo, and even Matanzas - are much more laidback, surf-oriented places to hang out.

Pichilemu, quite the hotspot for Chilean watersports, has been growing more and more popular with both locals (including nearby city residents) and international travelers since the 1980s. After the pandemic in 2021, even more city folk moved to the coast and adopted the seaside lifestyle, taking up surfing and/or kite surfing. Who can blame them?

The area's also home to Punta de Lobos - the famous lefthand pointbreak overlooked from the iconic Los Morros mirador, which was officially designated the 7th World Surfing Reserve in 2017.

Read more about Punta de Lobos, World Surfing Reserves and the Save the Waves organization on page 124.

LA LIGUA (I)

◆

If you prefer beaches to reefs, you'll like the Valparaíso region. Beach

resort **Los Molles** is one of the first you reach if coming from the north. Its horseshoe-shaped gray sand beach is backed by hills ideal for hikes. Needing a small to medium NW swell, it can produce powerful waves, suitable for all levels. Along La Ligua's protected wetlands, **Playa Pichicuy** - meaning small bay in Mapudungun - produces waves that are usually less powerful than Los Molles, perfectly suited to beginners on small swells. ◆ *All levels/ restaurants/easy parking.* ◆

MAITENCILLO (II)
◆

Playa Cachagua, in the seaside resort of the same name just south of Zapallar, is a consistent and exposed beachbreak, suitable for all levels. Works best during SW swells, can get crowded, and beware of rocks and currents. You'll have a view of Penguin Island while surfing.

In Maitencillo there are spots at either side of the rivermouth, **Abanico** and **Lagunitas**. They both work best at mid-tide on a SW swell. The wind can mess it up easily and it can get crowded. ◆ *All levels/sand/shower/toilet/restaurant/surf shop/surf school/easy parking.* ◆

VIÑA DEL MAR / VALPARAÍSO (III)
◆

Surfers have been going to **Ritoque** since the 1970s and it's still a popular break, especially in summer and at weekends. You can use the rip near the rocks at the northern end of the beach as an easy paddle out to the line-up. Works best on SW swells, there are lefts and rights to be enjoyed. ◆ *Intermediate and advanced/sand and rocks/shower/toilet/restaurant/surf shop/surf school/easy parking.* ◆

Beginner friendly **La Boca** has surf schools aplenty along its beach. Despite a tendency to close out, in the right conditions it's a fun wave, but beware of rips and currents. Best at low tide with a W swell. The further north you walk, the more likely it is you'll find better waves. The river can carry debris from nearby refineries. ◆ *All levels/sand/shower/toilet/ restaurant/surf shop/surf school/easy parking.* ◆

You'll seldom find **Reñaca**, or **Sector 5**, uncrowded, but it's very consistent and has several peaks to choose from; both powerful lefts and rights, and is favored by bodyboarders. Usually works throughout the tides and needs a SW swell. The beach has a heavy shorebreak as well as some localism - we recommend getting some local knowledge, treading with care and showing respect. ◆ *Advanced level/sand/restaurants/surf shop/surf school/busy paid parking during summer.* ◆

ALGARROBO (IV)
◆

In this area you'll find an option every hundred meters or so. Powerful left reefbreaks like **Tinajas** and **El Mejoral** all need a good S or SW swell, an advanced level and local guidance to surf them.

Along **Playa Los Tubos**, Deportivo - aptly named owing to its location in front of Club Deportivo Nacional - is where you'll find surf schools and a more beginner-friendly vibe. ◆ *All levels/shower/toilet/restaurant/surf shop/surf school/easy parking.* ◆

SANTO DOMINGO (V)

Playa Marbella, north of touristy Santo Domingo, is a dark sand beach where beginners and intermediates can try their luck. There's a surf school and parking's easy. Driving from town, you'll pass **Playa Rocas** and a point called **Terrazas** (which is worth a check, but rarely works - beware of rocks if it does). Other options are **Primera Roca** and **Segunda Roca** in front of the Santa Maria del Mar apartments. You'll have to walk from the car park of Santa Pizza parking to get there, and best to go real early, or in the late afternoon to avoid the wind.

MATANZAS (VI)

Caleta Matanzas and **La Vega de Pupuya** are beaches frequented by kite and windsurfers. When the wind's not too strong there are plenty peaks for all levels. Find restaurants and a surf school at Caleta Matanzas too.

Puertecillo is a favorite left for many surfers, so expect some crowds at times. You'll see the local groms

practicing some of their craziest manouevres here. Works best on a W / SW swell. Beware of strong current, rips and rocks. Drive further south to find a few quieter spots. ◆ *Intermediate and advanced/sand and rocks/easy parking/restaurant/surf school.* ◆

PICHILEMU (VII)

Surfy vibes all around in **Pichilemu**. Even if the peeps you meet in the water are not all 'local' locals, a good attitude and mucho respect is as welcome here as much as anywhere else. **La Puntilla** at Pichilemu can offer a long ride, use the channel wisely to get into the line-up - watching the locals before you jump in is recommended. Beginners can practice in the shorebreak and lessons are on offer at the surf school. Further south (and a challenging paddle to get to)

there's an advanced tubular left called Infiernillo. ◆ *Intermediate and advanced/ sand, reef and rocks/easy parking/restaurant/surf school.* ◆

Punta de Lobos isn't just a famous left-hand pointbreak and big wave surf contest site, more importantly it's a sensitive ecological habitat and

dedicated World Surfing Reserve since 2017. When it's BIG the waves break in front of the large sea stacks, obviously an exciting sight to watch! Although the smaller days are surfable too, they require an advanced level at least. Many pro surfer has moved here, so expect to see some phenomenal performance surfing out there. ◆ *Pro and advanced/rock/easy parking/ restaurant/surf school.* ◆

CHILE

SCHOOL RENTAL SHOP

◆

Longboards, shortboards, bodyboards, skimboards, skateboards and everything in between. **Waimea Surf Shop** (**130**) is one of the oldest and largest surf shops in this area and is the surfer's equivalent of a candy store. Needless to say, it's well equipped and has friendly, knowledgable staff. Besides surf essentials, and not-so-essentials that you don't-mind-having-anyway (like artfully-painted fins), they sell clothing and accessories. Open all year.

a. 11 Norte 896, Viña del Mar
t. +56 9 8970 9514
w. waimeasurfshop.cl

In the El Golf sector of Cachagua, the team of **Escuela de Surf Los Pinos** (**131**) offer lessons, rentals and surf trips. They've a café and surf shop too. Closed in winter.

a. Paseo Los Pinos, Cachagua
t. + 56 9 4103 9352 / 9 9322 8929
i. lospinossurf

Escuela de Surf Maitencillo (**132**) started their business in 2000, being one of the very first surf schools in Maitencillo. Expect a ton of experience and friendliness, and knowledge about surfing, the local area and the environment. On offer are surf and SUP lessons and rentals, and they have a little coffee shack providing drinks and snacks. Open all year.

a. Avenida del Mar, Maitencillo
t. +56 9 9885 6456
w. escualasurfmaitencillo.cl

Seres De Mar (**133**), founded and run by two local surfing brothers, can help you better your surf skills with coaching sessions, as well as offering normal surf lessons and board rentals. Open all year.

a. Avenida del Mar, Maitencillo
t. +56 9 5633 5762
i. seres_demar

Find surf school and café **Rapalón** (**134**) at the southern end of Avenida del Mar. Surf lessons, surf rentals and a great Açai bowl waiting for you after a hefty paddle. Open all year.

a. Avenida del Mar 121, Maitencillo
t. +56 9 6500 7855
i. rapalon_

Find the wooden shack of **Escuela Surf Lafkenche** (**135**) right at the beach, with individual and group lessons on the menu. Closed in winter.

a. Avenida del Mar 1300, Maitencillo
t. +56 9 9298 7410
i. lafkenchesurf

Find surf, skate, SUP lessons and rentals, and perfect coffee in their café, at **Beach House Maitencillo** (**136**). Open all year.

a. Sector 1 of Agua Blancas (Pajarera sector), Maitencillo
t. +56 9 4254 2943
i. beachhouse.maitencillo

Escuela Soul Surf (**137**) is set in one the typical wooden buildings in Concón. They've a dedicated team running a surf school, surf shop, climbing wall and a restaurant. The bonus? They've hot showers! Open all year.

a. Avenida Borgoño 24790, Concón
t. +56 9 8568 3836
w. escuelasoulsurf.cl

Along the same stretch of beach, in a similar wooden hut, **Escuela de Surf Chile Extremo** (**138**) offers surf lessons and rentals, and good coffees to start the day. Closed in winter.

a. Avenida Borgoño 23001, Concón
i. escueladesurfchileextremo

Besides surf and SUP lessons and rentals, **Escuela Punto Surf** (**139**) offers Polynesian Canoe lessons and workshops. Together with their knowledgeable team you can create a customized package that will fit your wishes, needs and level. Open all year.

a. Playa La Boca, Local 49, Concón
t. +56 9 5107 0595
w. puntosurf.cl

Pro Rider Surf (**140**) has lifestyle clothing and surf accessories, and offer lessons and rentals. Open all year.

a. Playa La Boca, Concón
t. +56 9 7800 2164
w. proridersurf.com

Surf and SUP school **Vivesurf** (**141**) rents out equipment too. They have a shop with all the surf essentials and a café on site. Open all year.

a. Avenida Carlos Alessandri, opposite nr 3028, Algarrobo
t. +56 9 4951 4614
i. vivesurf

Algarrobo Escuela de Surf (**142**) offer classes SUP and surf classes, as well as surf trips. They rent out equipment too. Open all year.

a. Avenida Carlos Alessandri, Sector Playa Los Tubos, Algarrobo
t. +56 9 7665 8361
i. algarrobosurf

Shaper Pablo of **Chaqual Surfboards** (**143**) does surfboard repairs, ever so handy when you're in the Algarrobo area and in need of a fix. But more importantly, he handshapes beautiful boards: longboards, fish, twin fins, all slightly alternative and classic boards. Best to contact through his Instagram. Open all year.

a. Algarrobo Area
i. chagualsurfboards

Find **Central Surf** (**144**) at the same place as Hostal La Tabla and their boulder spot. They've surf and skate lifestyle clothing and essentials. Open all year.

a. Avenida La Montaña 0721, El Quisco
t. +56 9 9698 3240
i. centralsurfchile

Escuela de Surf Costa Ventura (145) strive for the children of the community to have a place and connect with the sea and nature. So, besides surf lessons and surf coaching for both individuals and groups, they work together with the municipality and carry out social projects. Open all year.

a. Gran Avenida del Mar 026, Playa Marbella, Santo Domingo
t. +56 9 3417 2997
i. escueladesurf_costaventura

Surazo Surf School (146) is the surf school of Hotel Surazo in Matanzas but everyone is welcome to join their lessons or rent boards. Open all year.

a. Carlos Ibáñez del Campo, Matanzas
t. +56 9 9600 0110
i. surfschool_surazo

From the same owners of the surf hostel Puertezion, **Puertezion Surf School (147)** is situated right on the beach and hard to miss. Titan, who runs the school, is a well-known local with his heart in the right place, doing a really good job not just teaching clients to surf, but also teaching the local children surfing and sea knowledge. Open all year.

a. Playa Puertecillo
w. puertezion.com

Friendly and knowledgeable Elvis Marcelo Muñoz Rojas of **Manzana 54 Surf School (148)** offers lessons and rentals, and organizes surf trips too.

Their place is located close to La Puntilla, a beach perfect for learning. Open all year.

a. Eugenio Diaz Lira 5, Pichilemu
i. manzana54_surfschool

Close to Infiernillo, find **Tienda de Surf Back Side (149)** surf shop on the corner of Avenida Costera and Avenida Eugenio Suarez. Surf equipment and rentals. Open all year.

a. Avenida Costanera, Pichilemu
i. backside_tienda

At the south end of Playa Punta de Lobos, **Escuela de Surf Yampai Calfu (150)** offers group and one-to-one lessons with a certified coach, for everyone from beginners to advanced surfers. They also provide rental equipment. Open all year.

a. Punta Lobos, Pichilemu
t. +56 9 4680 0109
i. yampai.calfu

Escuela de Surf Molokai (151) offers rental equipment and surf lessons for both children and adults. Open all year.

a. Pasaje Punta de Lobos, Pichilemu
t. +56 9 8434 2393
i. molokai_escueladesurf

Another option for rentals and lessons from the surf school of the hotel - **Escuela de Surf Hotel Alaia (152)**. Open all year.

a. Camino Punta de Lobos 681, Pichilemu
t. +56 9 5701 5971
w. hotelalaia.com

SAVE THE WAVES - CHILE: PUNTA DE LOBOS

◆

The Save The Waves coalition have been looking out for surf ecosystems around the world for over 20 years. They identify, protect, steward, and defend areas where iconic waves overlap with important biodiversity and marine life hotspots. And, importantly, where local livelihoods depend on their preservation.

*"Put simply, a surf ecosystem is more than a wave -
it's the place, the plants and animals, and people."*

Enter Punta de Lobos, officially designated the 7th World Surfing Reserve in 2017. Known for its world-class surf and vibrant local culture, this famous left-hand pointbreak was one of the first waves in Chile to be consistently surfed by locals and visitors alike. Frequented by the world's elite surfers, we're talking about a wave that works in any conditions, from the smallest swell to XXL, has multiple sections which can connect to give long long lovely long rides - sometimes over 800 meters! - and hosts the Quiksilver Big Wave World Tour, El Ceremonial. Adding to this mighty perfect peak, the unique coastal landscape and rich marine ecosystem make it a truly special place. And overlooking the spot, the iconic 'Los Morros' mirador graces the point.

POWER TO THE PEOPLE
◆

Los Morros was saved from development by the community-led Fundación Punta de Lobos and their Lobos Por Siempre campaign, with thanks to the support of Save The Waves and Patagonia, the Marisla Foundation, Packard Foundation, Waitt Foundation and over 900 small donors. Having raised enough money to purchase the property, the group succeeded in conserving the biodiversity and landscape - the endangered native cactus can regenerate and thrive - and, pretty groundbreakingly, preserved public access forevermore.

Driving the campaigns and helping bring the community together for the years it took to achieve these goals, Chilean surf legend Ramón Navarro, Patagonia and Save The Waves Ambassador, says of his hometown: "It is where everything comes together in perfect harmony to create the most perfect waves on the planet and gives life to a unique natural setting. Punta de Lobos is an incredible marine sanctuary and it deserves to be respected and treated accordingly."

The son of a fisherman and diver, Ramón's childhood dream was to be just like his father. Until he discovered surfing. After meeting visiting surfers who inspired him to learn how to surf, Ramón traveled and surfed around the world until he figured out the best place to catch waves: right at home in Pichilemu. And having seen once pristine coasts that had been ruined by pollution and development while he was

traveling, he realized he could make a difference: "The coast that I loved so much was also under threat - from pulp mills, sewage pipelines, dams and senseless development. I know I have a responsibility to honor the generations before me by protecting the coast. I have to. It's up to us to make sure there are traditional fishermen (and fish) in the future. It's our responsibility to ensure our children and their children can see beautiful landscapes and biodiversity."

> *"Stand up to save some of these special places before they are gone"*

The many local fishermen who have made their living from its rich harvest for generations are aware how vital a biodiverse ecosystem is. The Humboldt current brings cold, nutrient-rich water to the area, creating the ideal environment for fish, crustaceans, sea lions, turtles, seabirds such as oystercatchers, penguins, boobies and pelicans, and a variety of whale species, from Orcas and Southern Right, Southern Sperm and Fin whales to migrating Gray whales. Ramón inspires and motivates action: "I know I can't accomplish much on my own. I think everyone sees the right thing to do: Stand up to save some of these special places before they are gone."

Save The Waves also worked with Fundación Rompientes to create the Piedra del Viento Coastal Marine Sanctuary, a 10,000-Acre sanctuary on the central coast. Now protected, the area's known for its scenic beauty and rich biodiversity, and holds six high quality surf spots, including the world class breaks Topocalma and Puertecillo. With the goal to protect 1,000 surf ecosystems by 2030, Save The Waves believes that the surfing community holds immense knowledge, passion and responsibility for the coastlines and surf breaks we visit, and aim to motivate and empower this international community.

Want to get involved? Support global coastal conservation, make a donation, join a fundraiser or campaign and help Save The Waves environmental efforts around the world.

w. savethewaves.org

SURFER'S EAR

On surfer's ear, Tom Carroll, earplugs, and why we should use them!

At least one of our team, and several of our friends, suffer from surfer's ear. Whether you're a coldwater surfer, or traveling and surfing a lot in waters that aren't all blue flag beaches, infection of the ears is a painful by-product of spending so much time in the water. Excessive exposure to cold water and air, or polluted waters – of which we're often unaware – can lead to ear problems and eventually to surfer's ear. Pursuing your passion can, in the case of frequently chasing waves, lead to bone growth inside the ear, narrowing the ear canal. It's a freakish thing our bones do, to try and protect us from the cold water, and it's called exostosis ('new bone' in Greek).

Once your ear canal's narrowed, it's harder to drain (sea)water, or dry out after a surf session. And since seawater isn't as clean as we'd all like it to be, and bacteria really appreciate the warm damp environment of your ear canal, the ear can get infected very easily. To protect your ears, and prevent developing exostosis, it's definitely wise to wear earplugs. SurfEars were developed by Swedish surfers (who happen to be product designers as well) looking for the perfect device to protect the ears from water, cold air and contaminants, but also let the sound in: a very important aspect of surfing, to stay balanced and connected to the surroundings. The development team of SurfEars worked closely with 2-time surf champ and waterman, Tom Carroll, to make improvements to their product. The result being earplugs that are truly experience-based and constantly tested, practical products, which work! They now use eco-packaging, and for a perfect fit; offer a wider size range in the improved SurfEars 3.0 and a modified size for young surfers (Junior SurfEars).

w. surfears.com

SEASIDE LOCAL: KRIS CABEZA

◆

If there's one thing that really stands out in the story of Kris Cabezas, it's his passionate drive to choose his own path. Being one of the first surfboard shapers in Chile, he had to navigate a few obstacles. But, to quote Franklin Roosevelt, 'A smooth sea never made a skilled sailor,' and the proof of his skill and knowledge show in the quality boards Kris shapes.

Born in the late 1970s in Southern California, his parents separated when he was still very young, so Kris and his younger brother, Ryan, were raised mainly by his Chilean father. They grew up surfing and skateboarding.

"My dad constructed swimming pools and did exterior landscapes, and he would take us kids along in the weekend if we didn't do our best in school. It kept us straight at school for sure, and also taught us to work with our hands from a young age. We used to take our skateboards, because the job's boring, and there was always an empty pool or a downhill driveway to explore."

It being a progressive place with regard to surfing and shaping, growing up in California meant a fair playground and plenty of opportunity to learn were on hand for the Cabezas boys.

"My dad, though, used to tell us that one day we all have to go and live in Chile. We grew up with all things Chilean, with the empanadas and all, haha, but we weren't keen on living there. I'd never even been there until my 18th! That year, turning 18 and being in my junior year in high school, my grandpa offered us to go for one month to Chile. It was August to September - the midst of winter in Chile. We arrived, and we went straight to the mountains to snowboard. Next, we took a bus to Antofagasta, to our uncle's house, who organized a trip to Iquique, and we surfed there. It was the first wave I ever surfed in Chile. Then we went back to Santiago where our grandpa put us on a bus south. And although that trip south bored me out of my mind at that age, I could appreciate its incredible beauty. When I got back to California, I thought, after my graduation I'm going back to Chile because it's insane!"

THE SANTIAGO YEARS

◆

And so he did. In 1986, after graduating, Kris traveled to Chile alone while his brother stayed in California to finish school. He stayed with his grandfather in Santiago, who offered him a job cooking. Landlocked in Santiago, the city life wasn't doing him any good.

"I wasn't digging it. I was missing out on surfing a lot. Then I started going to the beach and surfing in the weekends, driving to Constitución, to Puerto Maguillines, and camp out there."

"I'd brought 7 boards with me from the States - my family thought I was crazy, haha - but they were pretty battered. When my brother finally came over, he brought two new boards from California. We surfed these, and we were competing with them. Then we figured, these are our last boards; if we break them, there are no more boards for us to surf. The boards they were selling in Chile at that time were thin, rockered out boards mostly from Peru. And we were used to Californian boards, next level you know? After coming in second and third at a local contest, we bought two blanks in Iquique and created a little shaping room at the back of my grandpa's house. That's where we made our first boards, we each made a fish. We already knew how to do ding repairs and knew how to work with resin, but never really made a board. But growing up in Southern California where all the shapers were, and knowing a bunch of those guys, we knew a bit. And the fun thing was that the first boards we made, they actually worked! We competed with them. From then on, we started making more and my grandpa offered us a container we could work in."

SUPPORTIVE GRANDPA

◆

Meanwhile, Kris was planning to study in Santiago to become a chef. He likes to cook; his grandmother taught him, and he'd grown up surrounded by family members who cooked. His grandfather, however, being involved, supportive, and ready to teach his grandsons some responsibility, saw things for what they were.

"My grandpa said, 'You guys - you eat, breathe, sleep surfing, so just make surfboards!' He was going to California that week and going to go to Clark Foam. He made an order and came back with a container full of blanks. But he got really strict on how we could purchase them, and we had to figure out a way to pay him. I was 20 then, it's hard to run a business when you're that young and you just want to surf."

Another issue eating away at Kris was that he and his brother didn't want to live and work in Santiago anymore.

"We were in a pretty bad neighborhood. It was gnarly, things got stolen. We did make a few boards, and I went to Portugal that year - because I competed in the ISA games for Chile - and it was while traveling I realized that I needed to be at the beach."

They somehow found a way to convince their grandfather they needed to be by the ocean, surfing and trying out the boards, as well as selling them. He was fine with that, and so made a deal that he'd keep the foam blanks until they were able to buy them off him.

"He gave us five at a time and we were going back and forth between Santiago and Infiernillo, where we rented a house. And that's how we made our boards; from 1996 to 2000 we were making surfboards and all the while remaining to compete, surfing our own boards. That's also how we sold them - people buying them off us after the comps. And then people started ordering them, and little by little it started to become like a business. It was a fun time, we made a lot of interesting boards under the name Cabezas Bros, just signed with a marker. But like I said, being that young it wasn't easy to run a business."

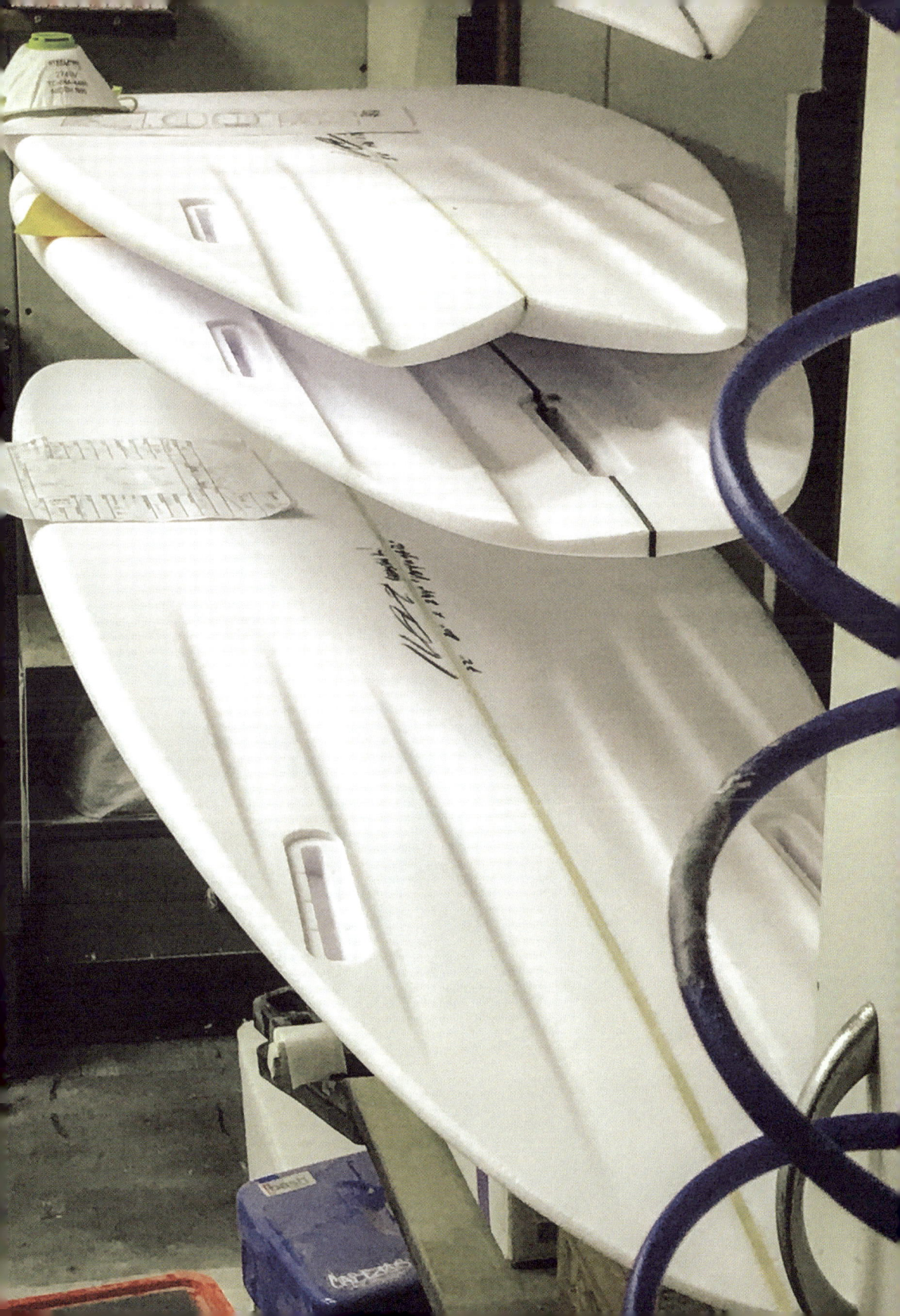

MENTOR TIMMY PATTERSON

♦

In 2000, Kris won a ticket to Hawaii in a competition. He traded it for a one-way ticket 'home' to California. He wanted to live and work there for a while. Traveling and doing the odd jobs for some years, he crossed paths with Timmy Patterson in 2006. Renowned San Clemente based shaper, Timmy Patterson started his board brand in 1980, having learnt the craft from his father and uncles, and was already shaping boards for some well-known champion surfers.

"I just met him one day and he said 'I'm working Saturday.' That was the next day, so I came by and sat there watching all these guys do their work, we chatted for hours. He asked me to work with him, back shaping, and I started the next Monday. He just threw me all kinds of boards that needed work. He would do one side, like do one rail, and then say 'Finish the other one.' He's so knowledgeable, and on top of that he's a really good teacher. I kept traveling now and then, to Japan, Costa Rica, and I always brought Timmy's boards. It was insane to have such nice boards on trips like that, then to come back and work with him again. I'm so happy for his success today. It's all down to the way he's been working, and his team. I'm still in touch with Timmy. Recently I learned a lot watching Italo Ferreira and the boards Timmy's been making him. Timmy's the mad scientist, giving Italo things to try out."

Around 2008, his beloved grandfather had a brain tumor removed, and didn't tell anybody about it. Kris unexpectedly got a call, 'You got to come back to Chile, your grandpa is in a coma'. He told Timmy he had to go back, and because of his grandfather's bad health he stayed in Chile longer than expected.

"I ended up going back to California to prepare to move back to Chile permanently. I noticed I loved it so much. Also, I'd learned tons from Patterson and I wanted to set up my own business in Chile. It was time. My brother said the same. It's time. My brother was still getting orders from people all the while. Timmy was cool with it and said 'You're off on this journey, you're going to need this, you're going to need that' like a mentor. I was just absorbing all this information, ordering a container and the tools I was going to need. I shipped the container to Chile and set off."

THE GOOD, THE BAD AND THEN THE BEAUTIFUL

♦

He went to Punta Lobos, built a factory, and worked there for many years. It was a good time, they were sponsoring children and holding events, shaping for the new generation. It was a great stage for both the young surfers and the Cabezas brand, because these kids were winning and making a name for themselves. They were good years. Until they weren't.

"I had to leave Punta Lobos at some point when things got a bit sour. My dad got seriously sick. It was difficult to see him like that because he's such a character, so strong. Unfortunately he passed away in 2016 and then there were legal issues with the property and I wasn't allowed to stay there."

Times were tough, even the working relationship with his brother changed, facing different work ethics. But his daughter was born in that same period.

"All the while I was roughing it, I was building the place here in Pichilemu where my kid can grow up safely and healthy. I got through it and was super stoked at the outcome and the new beginnings. Now I like to keep things small, in-house, have a small showroom. I've worked with a team and did large orders for big brands. It kept the wheel moving. But with the shifting dollar rate and risk, and everything

becoming so expensive... And the pandemic changed things too. My turn-around isn't as fast now that I work alone, but I trust in my boards, the quality, the way they work. I put a lot of thought in and use good quality materials. The surfing lifestyle here, certainly in comparison with my time in California, is very laidback. I have to admit, you get comfortable more easily and lose a bit of ambition and drive. My life now, here, is more like: if I can get some work done, then dust off, spend time with my family, and actually get some surf in, I'm stoked."

HANDSHAPE VS COMPUTERSHAPE

◆

Although Kris did a lot of computer work with Patterson, and he still has over 30 designs on file to maybe one day make with a computer, he now chooses to handshape. He likes the process better.

"You imagine what it will look like before you make it, and then somehow you try to work towards that. You can visualize the board you want to make and you've space to work, from that piece of foam, keep it simple, draw the lines out. Laminating is a skill - we've strong waves in Chile, so we have to focus on strong lamination - and sanding is a skill. I love sanding; you can bring the shape back that you had in mind that maybe after the laminating went a bit off. Like, get the rail sharp again, it's being born, you know? It's finally alive. Put a deck on it and you can go surf! While with a computer board you sometimes work backward; it's already cut to a certain shape, so you try not to change it. Handshaping may die off in the future, but not entirely. If the day comes where I have to do 50 boards, I will go back to machine shaping for that order."

DIFFERENT TIMES, DIFFERENT BOARDS, DIFFERENT SURFERS

◆

Chile is long past being behind on surfboard design and shapes. With a growing surf community and so many surf options along the endless coastline, the change in craft is inevitable.

"At the moment it's getting busier here too, the pandemic was an eye-opener for everyone. Apparently over 8000 people moved to Pichilemu, for example. Chile has high potential waves, north and south. Nowadays Chilean surfers are more curious, more open to try new things. There are a lot of nice Californian designs and high-performance boards coming in from Brazil, performance fish, retro fish, so this gets the local surfers curious. The attitude towards surfing - globally I'd say - used to be real serious, while now it's a bit more calmed down as in 'I'm going to go out and have fun'. The retro boards are more influential lately. The younger generation, the kids that are trying to compete, where we were years ago, they're looking for a performance feeling to surf their boards. The older generation, like me, we just want to ride, use a bigger board, feel looser, have more rail."

"We have the waves, you know, if you don't mind the cold. Our waves are long, there are so many sensations you can feel on a wave. So yes, like elsewhere you see a rebirth of fish, twinzers, Bonzers, single fins here too. There are plenty shapers out there now, playing around with fish shapes. It's also easier to shape a fish than a performance shortboard. I was always challenged to make the best high profile shortboard I could make. That's what I learned working with Timmy. But my first self-made board was a twin-fin fish."

"It would be wonderful if we could all turn to an eco-friendlier way of building boards, because, as we all know, surfboards are very toxic since the beginning. A very toxic item. I would like an eco-friendly resin to use. In the future, the petroleum-based items will get more expensive, forcing us to more conscious choices. I'm keeping a keen eye open and try to learn from what's happening."

◆

Curious about Kris and Cabezas Surfboards? Find him either at work in his shaping bay in Pichilemu, on the beach, or out surfing the breaks near Punta Lobos. **t.** +56 9 8134 7233 / **i.** cabezassurfboards

◆

FULL BODY STRETCH AND STRENGTHEN: PURVOTTANASANA

Reverse Plank Pose

A powerful pose, counterbalancing slouching and stretching tight shoulders and back.

Benefits:
Stretches the front of your body from shoulders, chest and hips, all the way down to the front of your feet. At the same time strengthening the back of the body, legs, arms and wrists.

How:
Start from a seated position with your legs straight out in front of you. Place your hands on the floor to each side of you, just behind your hips, fingers pointing forward. Squeeze the muscles in your buttocks, then push the hands firmly down while tucking your navel in (this helps engage your core muscles). As you inhale, start lifting your pelvis and roll your shoulder blades down as you lift your chest, keeping the back of your neck straight. It's quite an intense pose that's made *a lot easier* - but still provides all the benefits - if you keep your knees bent at a 90-degree angle. Stay here for a few breaths, engaging your whole back body and then slowly come back to sitting position.

Photo: Hotel Alaia

IN AND AROUND VICHUQUÉN

The further south you travel, away from Santiago and the more urbanized Valparaíso region, the more rugged the terrain. The Maule region has a coastal mountain range, fields of wildflowers, forests, dunes, wetlands, and river valleys where most of the population of this area live, herding and farming. Although it's very unlikely that you'll find drinks like kombuchas and plant-based lattes along this stretch, the seafood's fresh and the surf's pretty good too.

With its run-down pier jutting out into the sea and black sand beach that's backed by dunes and forest, Llico might be on your itinerary. Situated at the Llico river mouth, the end (or beginning) of Lago Vichuquén, the seaside village is a good place from which to explore the great outdoors - hiking, biking, surfing, kiting, paddling.

Long before the Spanish arrived, Inca and Mapuche had settled along the Llico river and Lago Vichuquén. At its borders sits a village with the same name, but when we say 'around Vichuquén' we refer to the lake, so much more room to roam. Having said that, a lot of land along the shores of the lake is privately owned and there's only one public beach. You can, however, drive along it and stop at many viewpoints. The town itself is built on top of an old Inca site and is a clear reminder of the Spanish conquistador days, with colonial buildings still intact. Beware (or rejoice!); the lake and its green surroundings are notorious for being gathering places for witches and sorcerers… If you look at the lake on a map and use some imagination, you can even spot the contours of a witch around its shape.

Following the tragic losses during the earthquake and tsunami of 2010, rules for how buildings should be constructed were introduced. Driving along the coastal road J-60, you'll pass caletas, inlets, that were once inhabited but the buildings haven't been restored, just a few ruins remain. Others, that either survived or were rebuilt, retain the timeless vibe of typical small coastal settlements. If you drive by Caleta Duao in the early hours, look out for the sight of many colorful fishing boats returning to their safe haven. And it may come in handy to know there's a gas station near Caleta Duao, in case you need to fill up, as there aren't many on the route.

If you're continuing your travels south down the Ruta del Mar from here, turn right onto the K-24 (also named 160) towards Constitución when the J-60 curves inland.

TO DO

♦

Explore the lake, its green surroundings, and the little islands and inlets from the water with **Nauti Tours** (**1**). They offer boat and SUP tours and rent out SUPs as well. While paddling, you can smell distinct whiffs of eucalyptus and pine, and try to spot the native shrub boldo. Boldo's considered a medicinal plant and is used to make tea that helps digestion (just so you know if you order it). Closed in winter.

a. Paula s/n Lago Vichuquén, Vichuquén
t. +56 9 7575 0155
fb. Nauti Tours

The town of Vichuquén's well worth a little visit. We say little, because the

town's tiny, so it won't take much time to stroll along the few streets lined with colonial houses and buildings - they're a declared Zona Típica, a national monument. At the town's entrance a witch holds guard, the statue referring to Vichuquén's nickname, Pueblo de las Brujas (Village of the Witches). Find out more about the myths, truths and history of this place at the **Museo Histórico de Vichuquén** (**2**). The museum holds artifacts of both Inca and Spanish colonial times. Open all year.

a. Manuel Rodriguez 332, Vichuquén
t. +56 9 8292 8991
w. fundacioncardoen.cl

Find the wooden shack of **Outdoor Vichuquén** (**3**) a few meters from

Llico's beach. Sebastian, who runs the sustainable activity center, will help you pick your favorite to-do from the offerings: surf or windsurf lessons, or hire fat bikes. Open all year.

a. J-80 981, Vichuquén
t. +56 9 4204 0381
i. outdoorvichuquen

EAT/DRINK/HANG OUT

♦

Hotel and restaurant **Puerto Viejo** (**4**) deserves a double special mention and is therefore listed in both our Eat and Sleep section. First of all, its sturdy yet elegant design with floor-to-ceiling windows, use of wood, metal and glass are a feast on the eyes. Their kitchen uses mostly local and seasonal food and wines, and there's

a good choice of meat, fish, vegetarian and vegan food on the menu. It's all deliciousness for very affordable prices, and the view from the restaurant is top-notch. Open all year. ◆$$◆

welcome pause if you're driving through. The name's a give-away for what to expect, the delight lies in the friendliness, the sweet empanadas (yes, sweet!) and choice of cakes that go so well with the coffee. Cozy inside, sea view outside. Open all year, Friday to Sunday. ◆$◆ ◆$$◆

a. J-60, Duao
t. +56 9 9300 0494
i. nenas.coffee

In a small street just off the J-850 find **Amelia Correa Cerámicas** (**8**). Amelia's ceramic creations are wannahaves. Her mugs, bowls, plates, pots and vases could fit in any tasteful interior magazine's photo pages; they look timeless, elegant, sturdy and simple. All pieces are handmade, and therefore unique. Open all year.

SHOP
◆

a. Ignacio Carrera Pinto s/n, Llico
t. +56 9 4440 3819
w. puertoviejollico.cl

Schop Home (**5**), located next to the lake, is a brewery pub serving quality craft beers. You can also get refills if you bring your own bottle. Every now and then, live music events are on the menu too. Lovely place and good spot to meet up with the local crew. Open all year. ◆$◆ ◆$$◆

a. Boulevard del Lago 3, J-830, Santa Rosa, Vichuquén
t. +56 9 9078 3254
i. schop.home

a. Quebrada Trilahue, Alto del Puerto, Vichuquén
t. +56 9 9714 4608
i. ameliacorreaceramicas

SLEEP
◆

Stock up on organic goodies, from nuts and grains to eggs and veggies, as well as freshly baked bread, sweet treats, vegan products and handicrafts at **Torca Organic** (**7**). Find the little shop in a wooden cabana on the roadside as you drive through Llico to the beach. Open all year.

As mentioned in the Eat section, hotel and restaurant **Puerto Viejo** (**9**) can be added to our list of favorites of favorites. The use of wood and steel is not uncommon in Chile, both being more earthquake-proof than any other material, and they do it so well. The rooms, built on poles, are positioned

Find **Nená's Empanadas and Coffee** (**6**) along the J-60, overlooking the beach just along from Caleta Duao - a

a. Avenida Ignacio Carrera Pinto Vichuquén, Llico
t. +56 9 8680 3551
fb. Torca Organic

in such way you've a free view over the ocean. And, a detail we particularly like, all rooms come with biodegradable toiletries. They have a spa, swimming pool, hot tub and lots of outdoor activities on offer. Open all year. ◆$$$◆

a. Ignacio Carrera Pinto s/n, Llico
t. +56 9 4440 3819
w. puertoviejollico.cl

Located at the lake, **Camping Vichuquén** (**10**) is a family and budget friendly basic campsite. The route towards the camping is a thrill in itself, driving a winding road down through thick forest. Sanitary blocks are a little outdated, but clean. They've a private beach, kayak rentals on offer and shaded pitches for tents and campervans, most located directly at the lake. Set in the middle of nature, expect a few (harmless) crawling creatures accompanying your nocturnal toilet or shower rituals. There's a small store and restaurant serving simple meals, dogs are not allowed. Open all year. ◆$◆ ◆$$◆

a. Lago Vichuquén, Camino El Mirador, Sector Oriente, Vichuquén
t. +56 9 3025 1948
w. campingvichuquen.cl

Hotel Parador (**11**) holds some treasures from yesteryears. It'd be easy to believe the hotel's been here since the colonial era, but it was built after the 2010 earthquake left the community in ruins. Holding the perfect balance by offering style and comfort with not too much fuzz - the

charm's in the details, such as the use of classic furniture and antique finds, cozy lighting and shady patios. They've 5 bedrooms with en suite bathrooms, a communal garden, restaurant, and a little souvenir shop selling local craftworks. Open all year. ◆$$◆

a. Avenida Comercio 329, Vichuquén
t. +56 9 3469 5639
w. paradorvichuquen.cl

IN AND AROUND CONSTITUCIÓN

Constitución sits on the mouth of the 240-km-long Maule River and was once the country's biggest shipyard and a popular seaside resort. On the 27th of February 2010, the city center was hit hard by the world's sixth strongest earthquake (8.8 mag), followed immediately by a tsunami which swept buildings and boats out to sea. Over 300 people disappeared that day, while years later, evidence of the disaster remains - empty plots of land, houses with cracks in their faces and a battered boardwalk are reminders of mother nature's power. The earthquake sadly coincided with Noche Veneciana - an illuminated riverboat show which is the highlight of the La Semana Maulina festival, a weekend of colorful activities held in February each year.

If anything, after their hardship and losses, the resilient people of 'Conti' seem to celebrate life harder and the festival's even more meaningful and magical these days. Almost all the locals have a story to share about how they survived that day, if you make time to sit and chat you'll hear some of them. And while Constitución may be a densely populated city with a strong cellulose smell wafting from its industrial pulp mill, its history and the surrounding areas - hills, valleys, dunes, and rock formations along the coast - make it well worthy of a visit. Add numerous black sand surf breaks hiding between the nature-sanctuary-come-national-monument-come-mind-boggling-rocks and sea arches, forget the city whiff, and you've found yourself in a remarkable region to explore.

TO DO

◆

Putú Dunes (12) might be the biggest dune area in Chile but that doesn't mean you'll come upon a signpost to help you find them - so make the dirt track discovery highway part of the adventure, why don't ya! While searching for an entrance to the dunes we met Carmen, a friendly local woman who makes an extra buck by asking visitors for a small fee when using her not-so-official-but-quirky-nuff-gate to enter the dunes. Or go with a trusted guide, who can not only lead you there but also help you spot (and avoid disturbing) the abundance of wildlife that live in this valuable ecosystem. Blown from the beach along 30 kilometers of coastline and shaped by the river, the huge banks of sand form a barrier between the ocean and mountains, leading to a series of lagoons and wetlands and a staggering meeting of landscapes. Eduardo Correa of **Maule Sorprendente (13)** promotes sustainable tourism and highlights the need to take care of the flora and fauna of this precious area. His tours range from 4x4 buggy adrenaline-seeker aventuras to peaceful discovering secrets tours on bike or foot. Open all year.

a. K-24, Cuchi, Constitución
t. +56 9 6668 8640
fb. Maule Sorprendente

Just a few minutes' drive from Constitución city, the **Museo de Sitio Cuevas de Quivolgo (14)** isn't the best tended but if you've any interest in caves and primitive times (and a little imagination), a wander along the walkways to this peaceful spot could transport you 4000 years back in time. Stone tools, ceramics, animal bones, seeds and ancient tombs were discovered in the caves, which are now a national archaeological monument. You won't find much beyond some info boards and some sculptures representing the ancient inhabitants of the caves but it's a muy tranquilo setting and one of the country's natural relics. Open all year.

a. Cuevas de Quivolgo, Unnamed Road west off K-24 at Quivolgo
fb. Cuevas de Quivolgo

If you're not feeling hikey yet are keen to stretch your legs and take in a view, a walk up **Cerro Mutrún (15)** (Green Lung) could be just the ticket. The 90-odd-meter-high hill trail's easily done in under an hour and the summit's a fine spot to sit and watch over the city, river, beach and Orrego Island. The start's signposted from the corner of the road where Bernardo O'Higgins turns into Avenida Enrique MacIver, no allocated parking just on-street. Accessible all year.

a. Cerro Mutrún, Constitución

All along Conti's seashore and the coastal road you'll pass plenty leg-stretching or let's-take-the-camera-out stops. Find sea-sculpted **stone formations** (**16**) resembling animals, buildings or whatever you make of them, like Piedra de las Ventanas and Piedra del León, close to the Maule river mouth. Along the M304 there's Piedra del Elefante, Piedra de la Iglesia and Piedra de las Termópilas.

And if you're traveling with children, climbing up and jumping down the wind-sculpted sand hill **Cerro de Arena** (**17**) might please them to bits.

a. M 304, Constitución

Take a trip along the river into the interior to see the rural side of the region on the last narrow-gauge train in Chile, the **Tren del Maule** (**18**) or Ramal del Maule. The train rides from Constitución to Talca and back, passing through a series of quaint villages and taking about 1 hr 20 mins each way. It's far from a regular ride (even if you already know what to expect on a train in Chile). If you're not up for the entire journey, you could opt for the halfway trip - get a return ticket to the González Bastías station, get off, shop around for some handmade treats and then hop back on the train as it heads home to Constitución. There are two train trips per day. Open all year.

a. Estación de Ferrocarril, Laureano González 1150, Constitución

After 20-odd years of some kinda tricky construction problems due to the unstable sandbed it was built on, and the loss of many workers' lives, the **Puente Ferroviario Bancos De Arena** (**19**) (bridge) was finally opened in 1915. The bridge, about 5 kilometers north of Constitución, enabled the train link across the Río Maule to Talca and was designed by Eiffel. Nowadays it's an engineering feat that you might be interested in if you're anything into err engineering. It's also a national monument and a fine feature for a selfie background, which you can cross on foot or bike. Accessible all year.

a. Puente Ferroviario Bancos De Arena, Constitución, Maule.

EAT/DRINK/HANG OUT
♦

Not exactly in Constitución, **Komo A Lo Pobre** (**20**) is, however, a highly recommended, amiable food stop-off just a short drive north of the city. They serve homemade lunch and dinner with veg options, and local craft beers. Open all year. ♦$♦ ♦$$♦

a. Aldea 450, Putú
t. +56 9 4292 0688
i. komo-alo-pobre

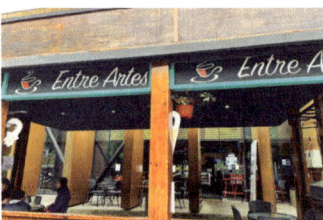

Entre Artes Cafetería (**21**) sits in the cultural center of Constitución, in front of the main plaza, and is a good place to meet locals and fellow travelers. The friendly staff serve cakes and pastries, sandwiches and picoteos (mini snacks), excellent coffee, fresh juices and milkshakes. People-watch from the terrace, or choose a table indoors, the set-up is simple, but inviting to chat. Open all year. ♦$$♦

a. Cruz 440, Constitución
t. +56 9 4285 1776
w. entreartes.cl

Another seafront lunch, dine or sunset drinks option is **Casa Del Mar** (**22**). A friendly, traditional kind of place, that also hosts weddings regularly, so best check beforehand so as not to be party-crashing anyone's best day! Open all year. ♦$$♦

a. Costanera del Mar 1434, Constitución
t. +56 9 5670 1696
fb. RestoCasadelMar

SLEEP
♦

Surrounded by cypress trees, glamping site **Sombras de Ciprés** (**23**) has a cozy peaceful feel and magical atmosphere. They've little sleeping domes and alpine cabins to rent, with

private hot tubs, a communal quincho (outdoor kitchen) with campfire area and a shared outdoor swimming pool too. Close to the Putú dunes and wetlands and only a 20-minute drive to the nearest beaches. Open all year. ◆$$◆

a. Aries de Culenco 1, Constitución
t. +56 9 7664 6694
fb. Sombras de Ciprés

Find **Hotel Playa El Cable (24)** hidden just outside the city, in the direction of the port, and right on the beach. Even though the town center's only a few minutes' drive away, here all's natural and tranquilo. Each simple but comfortable room has a private terrace overlooking the beach, they've an outdoor pool for leisure time, and wifi only in the lobby and restaurant area - a good chance to disconnect. The set-up isn't child-safe, so they don't accommodate children under 14; the upside (if you're not traveling as a family) is that it makes an extra quiet getaway for lovers

(and lovers of peace). Rooms are only for two people and it's one of the few hotels (if not the only one) with an ocean view in the city. Open all year. ◆$$◆

a. Playa El Cable, Constitución
t. +56 9 9458 2610
w. hotelplayaelcable.cl

A short drive south of Constitución, you can park your camper, pitch your tent, or rent one of the cabins or domos at the paradisical **Masi's Place Surf Camp Maguillines (25)**. The big bonus features are that Masi's a legend and it's only a short stroll from the camp to the surf right in front of you, the downside: we don't know how long he'll be able to

remain open due to some land issues with the authorities. So, check in with Masi to book ahead, hope for the best, and if the best becomes a reality; expect to make great memories at his place, and say hi from us! Open all year. ◆$◆

a. M-304, Constitución
t. +56 9 7245 8526
i. masis_place

Find **Ecoturismo Costa Blanca (26)** in the humble little town of Los Pellines, along the M-50 ocean road. Tucked into the dunes, close to the beach, they've spacious two-story cabanas (sleeping between 2-8 people) which are fully equipped with kitchen and bathroom, as well as luxuries like cable tv and hairdryers, and a camping area - all designed and built with love.

The campground has shaded pitches under the trees for camper vans (not really designed for mega motorhomes), a well-tended garden, big outdoor terrace and a quincho (outdoor kitchen) for guests. It's a safe and great place for families too, as long as you accompany children around the pool area. The lovely owner, Soledad, lives on the property and is more than happy to offer local tips and helpful info. Open all year. ◆$$◆

a. Blanca Estela s/n Costa Blanca
   Sector 2, Los Pellines
t. +56 9 5657 4277
w. eco-turismo-costa-blanca5.webnode.cl

IN AND AROUND CURANIPE
◆

Roughly 80 kilometers south of Constitución on La Ruta del Mar, Curanipe's considered the surf capital of the Maule region. You'll find a variety of surf breaks in relatively close driving distance between it and Pelluhue, and the small towns of Pullay. Named after its black stone in the native Mapudungun language, Curanipe was once an important seaport for the Cauquenes province and a popular coastal resort for the 'Cauquenes elite'. These days, the mix of traditional rural lifestyle and early 20th-century architecture combined with the steady development of hip lodgings make for a place you'd love to linger.

You'll also notice the area was badly affected by the earthquake and tsunami of 2010, with much of the infrastructure having been rebuilt since the disaster. 'The one that got away', however, is the abuelo amongst lighthouses, Faro Cabo Carranza, an iconic 1895 beacon situated some 40 kms north of Curanipe.

From the colorful boats at Caleta Curanipe, the fishermen's cove, and remote beaches such as Tregualemu to the rivers, lakes and lagoons that once thrived with Cauque fish (which the province is named after), you'll find forests meeting the coast and beauty spots like Arcos de Calán. Here, arches have been carved into the rocks by the ocean, creating a natural spectacle within the already remarkable landscape. Do stray inland off the coastal road to the small village of Chovellén. You can see men sitting outside their homes in a focused flow of weaving wool using sticks, with incredible skill and patience, following the tradition passed down through generations. It's meditative just watching them.

TO DO

♦

The mission at **Eco-Aventura Maule / Atipik Trip (27)** is to ensure you have an unforgettable experience and discover the region's wonderful landscapes with people who have a love for their land. Super-enthusiastic Arnaud (originally from France) works with a team of locals to promote conservation and support small business ventures and has lots of knowledge to share about native flora and all things natural. You've plenty options to explore the countryside and coastal hills: choose from a cart ride along the riverside to night walks and day treks, mountain biking and kayaking. Or learn some about the culture, traditions, gastronomy and customs of the south of Maule by joining their agrotourism initiative with the talented Cardonal weavers. Seasonal opening.

a. Calle Arturo Prat, Curanipe
t. +56 9 7382 7564
i. atipik_trip

Get up close and intimate with the birdlife and beauty spots of Río Chovellén on a kayak or SUP tour with **Curanipe Adventure (28)**. The wide and shallow, very picturesque river's calm enough for swimming so it's no adrenaline-junkie adventure, but add some cave exploring, canyoning or abseiling to your excursion if you've the need for some extra punch. Or ask them about a night-time paddle to see whether there's any truth in the name - Chovellén means Land of Witches in Mapudungun. Open all year.

a. VII región, Curanipe
t. +56 9 8432 0586
fb. Curanipe Adventure

Half an hour inland from Curanipe, you´ll find grand natural beauty **Saltos de Agua Quilicura (29)** at the end of a tricky road (that's worth the hairy moments). Holding top prize for the highest salto (waterfall) in the area, at 60 meters, you'll find more than one cascading, along with guided trails around natural pools suitable for bathing, a rope swing, picnic/BBQ area and hammocks. You'll meet the caretakers of the private reserve, Don José and his wife, Irene, at the entrance with their everyday smiles on, and have the chance to buy some of Irene's marmalade - sweet goodness, homemade with fruit straight from her huerto. If you've had an energetic hike and tackled the steep trails you can rinse off in the showers at the entrance next to the parking, there's also a cart where you can get some refreshments. Open all year.

a. Saltos de Agua Quilicura, Pelluhue (the paved road via Quilicura's the recommended route if you want to avoid too much forest trail dirt-track driving.)
t. +56 9 4053 8548

Another hike we recommend is the trek up to **Salto del Gato (30)**. Wear shoes that won't object to getting wet - every now and then you'll have to hop, skip - oops-missed - over and around, maybe through a few of the shallows along the Gato river. The water of the river falls freely off a 13-meter-high rock, creating a perfectly paradisiacal natural pool, that despite its icy cool temperature may feel oh so rewarding after your hike. The trek isn't signposted, so at all times keep the river close to avoid getting lost. Bring snacks and drinks, obviously taking all trash back with you. Expect to be out and about some 3,5 hours, be careful in winter due to the cold water, and at all times of the possibly slippery rocks.

a. Salto del Gato, Pelluhue

Seeing as the Maule valley's one of Chile's main wine regions we figure it'd be rude not to sample the goods while you're in the vino neighborhood.

Find centenary heritage vineyard **Viña Don Heraldo (31)** half an hour inland from Pelluhue, where owner Felipe's committed to making wine in the most sustainable way he knows how. Certified as 'APL' meaning Acuerdo de Producción Limpia (Agreement of Clean Production), they're minimizing their environmental impact wherever possible while making elegant artisanal wines, from the Cabernet Sauvignons and Carménères to the Carignan, which this area's renowned for. Check in for a tasting, guided tour, shop till you drop experience, stay to eat, or even book an overnight in one of their cabanas and sample the spa while you're there. Open all year.

a. Predio el Molino Lote H, M-820 Camino A Chanco, Cauquenes
t. +56 9 4226 6031
w. vdhwines.cl

EAT/DRINK/HANG OUT
◆

Lovel Van Cafetería (32) is a gem of a place, serving specialty coffees, juices, homemade pastries, veggie everythings - bagels, pizza, pasta, lasagna - and using fruit and vegetables from their own garden. And, who else has leaflets on the tables about birdwatching! And hand felted seabird decorations! Simply love this place. And if you love them too, you can opt to stay a bit longer and spend the night in one their wooden cabanas. Open all year. ◆$◆ ◆$$◆

a. Sector León Colgado s/n, Pelluhue
t. +56 9 7878 3704 / 9 9915 1741
w. lovel-van.cl

If you're in the mood for quality food, **Restaurante Terra Mar (33)** in Pelluhue could be your ticket to totally content. On the corner of a crossroads, with a terrace next to the sidewalk, their dishes are full of flavor, made from fresh ingredients and prepared with care. Choose from sandwiches to steaks or seafood, they've veggie dishes too and you'll do well to ask the friendly staff what the plate of the day is before you decide - it's usually a good choice. Open all year. ◆$◆

a. M-80-N, Pelluhue
t. +56 9 3205 0966
fb. Restaurante Terra Mar

Fancy some ceviche accompanied with a good old pisco sour? Beachside **El Grillo Restaurante (34)** is a modern-looking wooden-box-style place with a view of the caleta (fishermen's cove) and plenty of fresh fishy options. The portions are plentiful too and you can pay by card. Open all year. ◆$$◆

a. Costanera Ignacio Carrera Pinto 220, Curanipe
t. +56 9 8449 4337
fb. El Grillo Restoran

Hotel y Restaurante Punta Sirena (**35**) is located on the famous kite and windsurf spot it's named after, with a stunning ocean view. If you're up for a change of scenery with a little slice of luxury, want to get dressed up to go out-out, treat yourself to a cocktail and a fancy plate, you'll be impressed by their great food, friendly service and the clean modern style of the wooden building too. Reservations recommended. Open all year. ◆$$$◆

a. Sector Peuño Bajo, Pelluhue
t. +56 9 6779 8344
w. puntasirena.com

Find as much local goodness on your plate as possible at **El Chiringuito de Pullay** (**36**) where all veggies come straight from their huerto and they've a big emphasis on natural and healthy nourishment. Tucked away down a dirt road overlooking Tregualemu beach, the rustic and homely space is family and dog friendly, but small and cozy and pretty popular, so best book ahead or arrive early. And as with many places, you'll need to pay cash. Open in summer (January - February) and over weekends/holidays in November and December. ◆$$◆

a. Chiringuito de Pullay, Pullay
t. +56 9 1850 0344
w. puntapullay.cl

SHOP

ASAÍ Surf Café (**37**) is run by the extremely kind and positive Santiago and Cristina, who moved from corporate jobs in the city to the beach with their kids to start a new life by the ocean. Previously the shop of a close friend, they still sell their friend's handmade wooden art here, along with organic and natural goodies, which makes the place an eco store coffee stop combo. Originally from Brazil, Cristina makes the freshest, tastiest Acaí bowls, offering an enormous variety of toppings, as well as good strong coffee. And our favorite detail.. they're all about sustainable, honest products, making it a real feelgood place to shop. Open all year. ◆$$◆

a. M-80-N km 13280 Peuño Alto, Curanipe
t. +56 9 4264 7975
fb. Acai Surf Cafe

According to the local community and artisanal Maestro Queseros (Master Cheesemakers), the effects of the climate, terrain and salty air on the grasses growing in the marshes and meadows impart a special flavor and richness to the milk of the cows and goats that graze the area. Although you'll find Chanco cheese, butter and merkén in shops all over Chile, we don't think you can beat trying it straight from the source. For an authentic experience, find **Quesos de Chanco (38)** in a tiny garage-style shop, tucked away in a street on the coastal side of the village. Open all year.

a. Pedro de Valdivia, Chanco
t. +56 9 8255 8462
w. quesosdechanco.cl

SLEEP
♦

Hotel Puramar (39) is a modern boutique hotel with stairs leading straight onto the beach, offering accommodation ranging from standard hotel rooms to a private villa with spacious terrace that sleeps up to 8 people. They've two restaurants to choose from, fine dining at Puramar or casual at La Terraza, an extensive wine cellar, and outdoor pool and hot tub. Open all year. ♦$$$♦ ♦$$$$♦

a. Camino Curanipe, Pelluhue
t. +56 42 250 0510
w. puramar.cl

A very basic, but fine place to relax, connect with nature and play the guitar around the bonfire, **Camping La Ola (40)** is less than a kilometer from the coast and provides simple amenities such as picnic tables and a grill next to your camping spot, bathrooms, and a place to park. What else do you need when all that's on your mind is the morning surf check? They've pitches for tents and vans, small 'domos' that sleep up to 4, and private cabanas. Open all year. ♦$♦

a. M-80-N 545 Peuño, Curanipe
t. +56 9 9999 9695
fb. Camping La Ola

Already mentioned in our Eat section for a 'night out treat', **Hotel Punta Sirena (41)** is an eye-catching building with a relaxing atmosphere, offering all the amenities you expect from a modern hotel - outdoor swimming pool, hot tubs and a beautiful garden surrounding. They offer suites for up to 3 persons, and family rooms sleeping from 4 - 6. Open all year. ♦$$$♦

a. Sector Peuño Bajo, Curanipe
t. +56 9 6779 8344
w. puntasirena.com

Choose from a camping pitch, dome or cabin alongside the Chovellén River, close to the river mouth at the charming tranquil site of **Sirenazo Hostal (42)**. Each 'domo' is set on its own little wooden terrace, they sleep up to 6, are equipped with basic kitchen and bathroom, and have a view over the wetlands and river. The simple wooden cabanas also overlook the river, have two rooms - one double with bathroom, the other with bunk beds. A BBQ area and shared facilities are available for campers, they also offer activities, including surf, kayak, SUP, wind and kite surf lessons. Open all year. ♦$$♦

a. Rio Chovellén, Curanipe
t. +56 9 3190 3200
w. sirenazo.cl

If you're looking for a warm welcome and friendly vibes, a stay at **Ecolodge Ekilibre (43)** provides just that, as sustainably as can be. This family-run eco hostel belongs to a French-Chilean couple, Stéphanie and Germán, their son Noah and their cat. This ongoing project in low-impact hospitality means a compost toilet along with water and energy saving systems, has a double room, a family room for up to 4, and a bunk room with 6 beds and big bright open kitchen, sunny living room, and spacious outdoor terrace. Set in the fields a couple of kilometers south of Rio Chovellén, you can hear the sound of the sea and get plenty of tips about surfing in the area from Germán, who's been surfing most of his life. Open all year. ♦$♦ ♦$$♦

a. Jose Rivas Hernandez, Pasaje A s/n Sector Cardonal, Curanipe
t. +56 9 8406 4596 / 9 9877 8780
i. ecolodge_ ekilibre

Built from scratch in innovative style (using recycled and natural materials like mud and wine bottles and suchlike brilliant construction) by its owner Arnaud, **Casa Atipika** (**44**) seems the perfect name for this very atypical but charming place. The quirky design might look odd but once you arrive you'll feel right at home, whether you rent a room in the house or one of the cabins. Originally from France, Arnaud's also the owner of Eco Aventura Maule (see To Do section), and is full of energy and enthusiasm for the land that he now lives on - ask him anything about the area to be amazed by his knowledge and how much love he feels for his Chilean home. He makes the best breakfasts and runs a sociable joyful place, ideal for budget backpackers who want to mingle around the fireplace with other guests at night and share some stories over a beer. And you'll likely have company for a walk to the beach, as his rescue dogs will be keen to follow you along for any adventure. Open all year. ♦$♦ ♦$$♦

a. Jose Rivas Hernandez, Pasaje A s/n Sector Cardonal, Curanipe
t. +56 9 7382 7504
fb. Casa Atipika

Family-friendly surf camp **Puntas del Maule** (**45**) offers camping and 2-person basic cabins on stilts, or a stay in the 'refugio' - a 3-level shelter with its own BBQ area and clay oven, kitchen, bathroom and double/twin bedroom. They've all kinds of optional activities for adults and children, from full surf experience lessons or guided trips, to yoga, dance and meditation classes. You can also learn and get involved with agriculture in their orchard and greenhouse, join a trek or birdwatching tour, or opt for quiet time and enjoy an outdoor bath under the stars. Located 300m from the beach with a lush garden surrounding them, find the camp a few kilometers south of Rio Chovellén. Open all year. ♦$$♦

a. Lote 2A, Sector Quilicura
t. +56 9 7793 7745
w. puntasdelmaule.cl

Camping at **Punta Pullay** (**46**) is a great location for easy access to the surf, right in between the surf spots of Curanipe and Buchupureo/Cobquecura. They've basic camping pitches in the countryside, an onsite restaurant (Chiringuito de Pullay - see Eat section) and optional activities available. Seasonal opening.

a. Chiringuito de Pullay, Pullay
t. +56 9 1850 0344
w. puntapullay.cl

RESTORATIVE POSE: ARDHA MATSYENDRASANA

Seated Twist Pose

Twist it out. A gentle and easy pose to give your spine some love, and a break from repetitive movements (or no movement at all).

Benefits:
Enhances spinal mobility, stretches shoulders and chest, the outer thighs. Can relieve lower back pain, and aids your digestive system.

How:
Start in a seated position with both legs stretched out in front of you. Lengthen your spine and bend your right knee towards your chest. Place your right foot on the inside of your left thigh, wrap your left arm around the outside of the right knee, and place your right hand behind you. Keep the left leg active by pointing the toes up. On each inhale try to lengthen the spine, and on your exhale, gently twist a little deeper by gazing over your right shoulder. Make sure your buttocks stay connected to the ground. For a deeper stretch, place your foot on the outside of the thigh. Stay for a few breaths then do the same on the other side.

IN AND AROUND BUCHUPUREO AND COBQUECURA

◆

The Ñuble region is another land of contrast with its black sand beaches and green landscape. Despite increasing numbers of visitors and incomers buying property along this coast, the pace of life remains easy around the seaside towns of Buchupureo and Cobquecura. The vibe is tranquilo and you'll see cowboys on horses (huasos) wearing traditional outfits. On the oceanside, you've a chance to share the stage with all sorts of marine life - birds, sea lions, cetaceans such as sei whales, orcas and dolphins.

Buchupureo, or Buchu as the locals call it, is a laidback and not a lot going on besides fishing and farming little town. Part of its magic is the lefthand pointbreak, La Boca - far from a secret among the surfing community and yet, one of the few surf spots on the planet to hold onto its unique mellow soul. To its south, the rocks form majestic natural monuments which have graced the area for over 200 million years - known as La Piedra de la Ventana, and Iglesia de Piedra (Stone Church) due to the light playing through the huge 'windows' and a 'Virgin' sculpture inside it. A few kilometers further down the coast, the larger town of Cobquecura, (meaning Stone Bread in Mapudungun) is where you'll find ATMs and the like. You can also ramble around the quaint fishermen's cove and get an accurate representation of 19th-century Chilean architecture in the historic center, where work continues to repair the buildings after the 2010 earthquake.

TO DO
◆

Cobquecura Piedra de La Loberia (47) is a big rock in the bay of Cobquecura which provides a sunbathing-snoozing platform for a colony of around three thousand lobos marinos - sea lions. Bring your binoculars for a 'National Geographic kinda experience' and hear the roars, barks, growls and grunts as they flollop about, vying for space. If you watch a while, you'll notice some losing their spot on the rock after going for a swim - as the Chileans say, 'El que fue a Melipilla perdió su silla' - the one who went to Melipilla lost his chair. The site's an official Nature Sanctuary with the ocean forming a natural barrier between lobos and spectators and is an extra spectacular sight at sunset. Accessible all year.

a. Piedra de la Loberia, Cobquecura

Learn some about the history and heritage of the town on a guided tour at **Ecoturismo Museo Cobquecura (48)**. The eco-museum helps to promote and conserve the culture and traditions of the region, and has an area dedicated to Chilean Nobel prize-winning poets born in the town. On the patio you´ll find native plants and fruit trees such as tomatoes, and (due to the microclimate) tropical varieties like papaya and passion fruit. On-street parking outside, free entry - donations gratefully received. Part of the house was transformed into a hotel, so you've the option to stay the night if it suits (see Sleep section). Open all year. ◆$◆

a. Independencia 98, Cobquecura
t. +56 9 9632 5308
w. ecomuseocobquecura.com

A few kilometers inland from Buchupureo, find gentle treks and magical viewpoints at **Parque Las Nalkas (49)**. The 22-hectare native forest reserve is a jungle-style tree-filled ginormous-leafy-plant-packed little wonder, with paths suitable for children and flip flop strolls. Your feet might appreciate some proper shoes for the steeper climbs and the tree swings, but the 1-maybe-2-hour path (guided by wooden signs) isn't strenuous. There's a small entrance fee and a cafeteria-pizzería close to the entrance. They also have boutique hotel quirky cabins if you want to stay longer than a wander. Open all year.

a. Talcamavida 3.5 km, Buchupureo
t. +56 9 3897 8765
w. nuevo.parquelasnalkas.cl

If you're visiting in winter and keen for a surf and ski/snowboard combo, find **Centro de Ski Nevados de Chillán** (**50**) about 3-hours' drive from Buchu. Previously known as Termas de Chillán, famous for the thermal pools, it's now well known as one of the best ski resorts in the country, with more than 20 slopes - including the longest one in South America, the 13-km-long Las Tres Marias.

If you're here in summer you can hit the trails of the bike park (rental bikes and equipment available), pump track, and/or zip through the tree canopy. You'll also find a thermal water park, spa, climbing wall, and accommodation - camping for campervans or the choice of 2 hotels. Seasonal opening.

a. Camino Nevados de Chillán km 85, Pinto
t. +56 44 335 0004
w. nevadosdechillan.com

EAT/DRINK/HANG OUT

◆

Get your specialty coffee and really anything dough at **Café La Mano** (**51**). On top of their selection of delicious cakes and baked goods (most from 'masa madre' - sour dough) this colorful funky little stop also serves gourmet pizzas, sandwiches and pastries, and has plenty plant-based options. Open all year. ◆$$◆

a. Sargento Aldea, Buchupureo
t. +56 9 6310 5799
i. cafelamanocl

El Puerto Buchupureo (**52**) is a big vibrant restaurant with a great terrace. Full of plants and decorated with Tibetan flags, foreign licence plates and the like. The menu doesn't surprise but they offer affordable good quality food, a stone's throw from town, on the beachfront (where the new boulevard's being constructed). It gets crowded during summer, so if you're in a hungry rush and want to gauge how long the wait will be, check the parking lot; if there's no space it's a good indication that the terrace is jam-packed too. Open all year. ◆$$◆

a. Camino Cobquecura km 8, Cobquecura
t. +56 9 9161 2315
i. restauranteelpuertobuchupureo

Oh how we like this place! **Restobar Cerveceria Cofke** (**53**) is the beer garden of Cobquecura, hidden down a residential street. As soon as you set foot in the bar-restaurant you'll appreciate its vibe - decorated with motorbikes and surfboards, which create a Deus Ex Machina kinda feeling. Offering a grand selection of craft beers straight from their own brewery in the backyard and a pub-food menu (including veggie burgers that taste better than the meaty ones - give them a try if you doubt our tastebuds). Portions are generous, the staff are super, and you can stop for a bite with your whole family, doggos welcome too. If you're after a nightlife bar partyfun check it out at night over the weekend. Salud! Open all year. ◆$$◆

a. Alcalde Barrios 528, Cobquecura
t. +56 9 7532 7707
fb. Restobar Kofke

You can expect personalized service, great flavor and exceptional wine pairing, along with a beautiful view over Playa Rinconada, at **Ruka Antu EcoLodge** (**54**). Their Peruvian chef and sous chef take pride in using fresh local products wherever possible and have a real flair for making traditional food with a modern twist,

and supporting a circular economy. Treat yourself to something beyond your typical go-to-while-traveling dish and soak up the atmosphere at this modern-rustic resto-bar, then finish off with a pisco-something. See Sleep section for more info. Open all year.

◆$$$◆

- **a.** Camino Colmuayo Mela no. 18, Cobquecura
- **t.** +56 9 6811 0895
- **w.** rukaantu.cl

SHOP
◆

Follow your nose to find the fresh baked goods of **Panaderia Artesanal Trigo Negro (55)** in most of Buchu's minimarkets. Supplying shops and eateries in the area with more than 'masa madre', they also create great artisanal twists on famous European breads like French baguettes and Italian focaccia. Open all year.

- **a.** Buchupureo
- **i.** trigonegropanaderia

Ecostore **Las Cabras del Monte (56)** on the main square of Buchu is easy to overlook due to its small size, but once you set foot inside it'll be hard to leave empty-handed. From local arts and crafts to vegan goods, herbal teas and sweet treats, handmade soaps, cruelty-free cosmetics and eco-friendly cleaning supplies, and some surf accessories too. Open all year.

- **a.** Diego Portales 33, Buchupureo
- **t.** +56 9 8583 7794
- **fb.** Las Cabras del Monte

Get a real feel for the local handiwork skills by taking a drive into the capital of Ñuble and wander the streets of the **Feria Artesanal de Chillán (57)**. Just over an hour's drive from the coast, Chillán's renowned for being one of the most important artisan centers of the country and holds the street market and craft fair every day, attracting people to browse from far and wide. Find locally grown produce and street food stalls, along with handcrafted goods from local artisans and the rest of the country. Even if you're not a big shopper, to soak up the atmosphere, smell the culinary delights all around and admire the wares, you'll find plenty of variety - from leather, stone, wool and wicker, to basket weaving, the woodcarvings of Coihueco and the famous clay pottery of Quinchamalí. Open all year.

- **a.** Plaza Sargento Aldea, Chillán

SLEEP

Named after one of Chile's commonly seen birds (the Southern Lapwing) **Queltehues Eco-Camping** (**58**) has ten spacious camping spots, also named after different feathered beauties. This incredibly quiet spot with a relaxed set-up is next to a river, with a huerto, deck chairs and hammocks, kayaks to use and a shared modern-style wooden clubhouse to hang out, work or prep some food. All spots have a picnic table and firepit, with optional sink and electricity spots available. Heaven for all; solo travelers, couples, families, and dogs too - it's basically one safe playground with a dawn bird chorus. No need to drive or walk to the surf either, you can paddle downriver about 200m to the ocean. We recommend booking in advance, as this is becoming a favorite escape and only has a few spots, to keep the magic spacious vibe. If you go, please say hi to sweet owner Gabriela and her two amazing sisters (who all live on the grounds). ♦$♦ ♦$$♦

a. Sector La Boca km 8.8, Buchupureo
t. +56 9 3254 6455
w. queltehuesecocamping.cl

On the hill above the beach of Buchupureo, **La Joya del Mar** (**59**) boutique hotel offers 3 fully-equipped holiday villas (each sleeping up to 4 persons) in a luscious well-maintained garden. In addition to the swimming pool and big hot tub overlooking the

ocean, you'll often find American owner Chris enjoying the grounds - if he's not enjoying the waves, of course. In the main house, find restaurant La Joya, serving tasty homemade food and a great papaya sour. Open all year. ♦$$$♦

a. Camino Buchupureo km 8.5, Cobquecura
t. +56 9 8632 1900
w. lajoyadelmar.com

B&B **Casona Cobquecura** (**60**) also houses the Ecoturismo Museo Cobquecura and gives a real community feeling as your stay helps support the project. It's a small 5-room accommodation with simple but decent facilities, tasty breakfast with freshly baked bread, which you can enjoy in the garden with your morning coffee and juice. On cold days the central heating keeps you cozy but have no fear of settling into a work routine while you have a roof over your head - the internet only works in the reception area. Open all year. ♦$♦

a. Independencia 98, Cobquecura
t. +56 9 9632 5308
i. casonacobquecura

Also mentioned in the Eat section, prepare to feel a little stunned by the

beauty at **Ruka Antu EcoLodge** (**61**) where wood and glass meet vases filled with wildflowers and an ocean view. The design manages to feel modern and stylish at the same time as natural and comfortable, creating a relaxing surfy vibe. Each room has a private terrace, most with a view over Rinconada beach. On top of the good vibes and seaside décor, every member of staff you meet, from reception to waiting staff and even the cleaner, will give you a warm welcome and take really good care of you (without overdoing it and making you feel they're hovering above you). Open all year. ♦$$$♦

a. Camino Colmuayo Mela no. 18, Cobquecura
t. +56 9 6811 0895
w. rukaantu.cl

Rinconesia (**62**) is an eco-camping site in front of Rinconada's beach, with basic facilities but only a short walk to the surf. Slightly outside town, so there's not much around except a small self-built 'amphitheater' where you can sit round the fire and listen to music in the evenings. Part of the Familia Surf company, you can also rent one of 4 beach-view cabañas, (sleeping from 2 to 8 persons) and organize adventure activities with them, or join a beach clean - pura vida! Open all year. ♦$♦

a. Sector Rinconada, Cobquecura
t. +56 9 8903 1241
w. rinconesia.cl / familiasurf.cl

IN AND AROUND CONCEPCIÓN AND THE COAL COAST

The Biobío region's 'coal coast' is thick with mining history, rich with traditions, and the diverse landscape often met with colossal stormy swells, while scarred with remnants of bygone earthquakes and tsunamis. Often humid and rainy, the evergreen Araucaria trees and cinnamon trees do well in the native forests, where puma, culpeo foxes, South Andean deer (pudú) and vizcacha (rodents related to the chinchilla) thrive.

As you enter the northern province of Concepción you'll notice that you're leaving the swathes of untouched nature behind and might even feel a little cosmopolitan tremor as you approach the region's capital city, which the province is named after; Concepción, or 'Conce' as the Chileans refer to it. Sitting alongside the Biobío rivermouth, this busy port is the second largest city in Chile, so you can expect some industrial vibes, heavy traffic and pollution. But it's also known as the country's capital of music, which means if you've a thirst for music, museums, art, nightlife and barhopping, you'll find a vivid scene, especially around the university district.

There are, however, still heavenly little pockets dotted around for those willing to take a short trek, don't you worry. Only half an hour north of the city, El Túnel - a 3 km walk south of the parking for Playa Punta de Parra - offers total respite from city vibes with its long stretch of white sand, green backdrop and sparkling clear water. To the southeast, Parque Nacional Nonguén meets the suburbs. Meeting the city's southern edge, Laguna Grande San Pedro affords tranquil calm for water enthusiasts when the city and stormy sea are less than inviting.

Traveling south from Conce down the coal coast takes you through the Arauco province to explore the spots around Lebu and Tirúa, then into the Araucania region. The Mapuche of this area, 'Araucanos', fly their flags and hold onto their rights and lands with determination and pride, and due to a long history of unrest between the Chilean state and the Araucanos, some of these areas are (at time of printing) considered high risk zones. While it's unlikely that you'll be getting involved in any conflict as a traveler passing through, the situation can create an uneasy vibe at times, and one that you should be aware of. If you have enough up-to-date knowledge of the area there's incredible nature and the chance to learn about the fascinating culture and lifestyle of the 'people of the earth'. However, if you're going south and don't have time to check the current status of the area or prefer to just zoom by without any risk of incidents, inland highway Ruta 5 Sur will see you from Concepción to your next destination.

TO DO

Parklife and green green grass can be found in the grounds of **Concepción University Campus** (**63**). Chill under the shade of a tree, admire charming architecture (and even a duck pond), dance, siesta your head off, people-watch to your heart's content at this popular hangout. Free entry to the public, day and night, accessible all year.

a. Campus Universidad de Concepción, Concepción

Facing Plaza Perú, within the university campus, the museum **Casa del Arte José Clemente Orozco** (**64**) is otherwise known as Casa del Arte

or Pinacoteca. Holding the most complete Chilean painting collection in the country, with over 1800 works from different eras representing Chile's history. Find permanent exhibitions and rotating installations, works from the great masters as well as modern art. In the entrance hall, the famous mural 'Presencia de América Latina', painted in 1964 by Mexican artist Jorge González Camarena, draws the crowds. Free entry, open all year.

a. Avenida Chacabuco 1343, Concepción
t. +56 41 220 3835 / 41 220 4419
w. extension.udec.cl/pinacoteca

It's only a few minutes out of town but Laguna Grande San Pedro de la Paz feels far removed from the city with its still water and peaceful calm

green surroundings. Enjoy the beauty on a paddleboard or kayak with **SUP San Pedro** (**65**) and ask them about their Yoga SUP combo option, sunset sessions available too. Open all year.

a. Laguna Grande San Pedro, San Pedro de la Paz
t. +56 9 7681 0674
i. sup_sanpedro

West of the city find the **Desembocadura Natural Park** (**66**). Over 500 hectares of native coastal forest on the Hualpén Peninsula provides a stunning scene for the Desembocadura (rivermouth) break. There's a small entrance fee to the park itself but if you're here only for the surf you pay half the fee to enter. But err, don't forget the pollution mentioned above if you fancy surfing city breaks.

a. Rio Calle Calle, Hualpén

Just under an hour's drive south of the city, the botanic garden at **Isidora Cousiño de Lota Park (67)** feels a bit of a surprising contrast to the normal scenery with its French style and sculptures. The 14-hectare park was built by an Englishman back in the 1800s, when wealth was obtained from coal production in the area. The privileged position of the park (in front of the seashore) makes it a seaside approved 'to do'. Small entrance fee, open all year.

a. Avenida El Parque 21, Lota
t. +56 41 287 1022
i. parquelota

Every now and then we stray way away from the seaside because there's something, a place, just as mesmerizing as the ocean. Lakeside town **Pucón (68)** is known as Chile's adventure and outdoor heaven. With its view of snow-covered Villarrica volcano and activities such as skiing, canyoning, rafting and kayaking, it's quite rewarding to swap salty air and cold water for hot springs and microbrews for a bit. Microbrews? Well yas, find hipster bars to five star lodgings. Although a few hours' drive from the ocean, it's not off the beaten path; it's a popular destination for both the well-to-do tourist and intrepid backpacker year-round. Activities can be as challenging as hiking up the

volcano with ice axes and crampons (you need a local guide to take you up) to checking out waterfalls and splashing around in thermal baths. Although the tub will be crowded in summer!

a. Pucón

EAT/DRINK/HANG OUT
◆

In the mood to put on some bling and treat yo'self to a fancy lunch? **Punta de Parra Restaurant (69)** has a classy atmosphere (maybe drop the 'yo's, yo) with a beautiful sea view, black and while tiled floor, wind screens and shiny parasols. Seafood, anyone? Open for lunch at weekends and during holidays, and it's a hotel restaurant so if you want to really splash out, check their accommodation options. Bling bling ka-ching! ◆$$$◆ ◆$$$$◆

a. Punta de Parra, Tomé
t. +56 9 5609 0086
w. puntadeparra.com

Downtown **La Cocina (70)** is a family-run restobar that's been getting more popular every day for the almost three decades that it's been open. This buzzing hotspot with a welcoming interior and big outdoor terrace opens its doors at 8am for breakfast and doesn't close them till the after-midnight nightcaps are drunk. If you order one of the 35 different mojitos it'll be garnished with fresh mint from their own huerto. Doing everything possible with eco-friendly everythings from composting to recycling, and fickle minxy whatnots like plastic straws were banished long ago. Add some great music and big shareable portions of food, then top it off with a sweet story - the mural of the dog on the wall outside is famous in Conce for bringing luck to those that touch her head. You'll likely see a few students coming to give her a pat if you're there during exam times. Give it a try, what's to lose! Open every day, all year. ◆$$◆

a. Avenida Paicaví 246, Concepción
t. +56 41 223 5658
fb. La Cocina

Going for a 'picada' means exactly what you get at **Fuente Penquista (71)**. It's no-nonsense place where you can grab a bite. The food's good at a good price and you can sit at the bar to watch it being prepared. A cozy spot for a weekday lunch, it fills up quickly. Open all year. ◆$◆

a. Libertador General Bernardo O'Higgins 63, Concepción
t. +56 9 5772 8491
w. fuente-penquista.negocio.site

High quality Arabic freshly roasted coffee, freshly baked bread and pastries and simple 'suggestion of the day' dishes are on offer at **Tostaduría de Café Coyoacán (72)**. And they've vegan and gluten free options aplenty. Open all year. ◆$◆

a. Avenida Chacabuco 1111, Concepción
t. +56 9 8739 1054
w. tostaduriacoyoacan.cl

Lo que más quiero (73) means 'the thing that you most want' but how to decide what that is. Dish of the day. Good quality wine. A refreshing cocktail. Maybe they should change the name to 'everything that you most want'. And err in the meantime, just order everything on offer. Open all year, weekdays only. ◆$$$◆

a. Lincoyán 60, Concepción
t. +56 9 3949 1859
fb. Lo que más quiero

In the music capital of Chile, **Casa de Salud (74)** serves it up with a lively mix of live bands and DJs, from small to large, jazz, pop, house, techno. Open all year. ◆$$$◆

a. Brasil 574, Concepción
t. +56 9 4427 8100
w. casadesalud.cl

In recent years, plant-based places have started popping up in Conce like poppies and **Govinda's Vegan Concepción (75)** is a tall bright one. Serving tasty portions at a reasonable price, we can recommend getting a takeout to eat alfresco at nearby Parque Ecuador, enjoy some plants while being surrounded by... uuh plants! Open weekdays for late brunch, lunch, snacks, all year. ◆$◆

a. Cochrane 214, Concepción
t. +56 41 279 5911
fb. Govinda's Vegan Concepción

Olas de Tirúa (76) is across the river from its town (Tirúa) and offers a stunning view, especially at sunset. The decor's colorful, the vibe's a fun one, food's great (stone oven pizzas deserving of a special mention), the owner speaks English, and international credit cards are accepted. And if you can't walk after an evening on the terrace filling up on good food and wine there's a stayover option too. Open all year. ◆$$◆

a. Km 1 Camino Puntilla de Tirúa, Tirúa
t. +56 9 8205 9507
fb. Olas de Tirúa

SHOP

♦

The **Feria Internacional del Arte Popular** (**77**) is the biggest art fair of the country, with over 130 national and international exhibitors. Besides art and crafts there's live music, dancing, food and good vibes aplenty! The market is held annually, from late January to early February.

a. Parque Ecuador, Víctor Lamas 567, Concepción

Light, colorful and pleasant are the first things that come to mind when thinking of **Hostal Boutique Concepción** (**78**), located in the buzzing heart of the city. This is a place where all kinds of travelers meet. Rooms are basic bunk rooms but neat, sleeping solo travelers, couples, friends and families. Open all year.
♦$$♦

a. Ongolmo 62, Concepción
t. +56 41 318 9308
w. hostalboutiqueconcepcion.com

For a real breakaway, book a stay at **Pura Lodge** (**79**) and get a jaw-on-the-floor view of the Lagune de San Pedro de la Paz. Surrounded by water and endless green, with not a sound but those from nature, it's hard to believe the city center's such a short drive away. The enormous, gorgeous rooms have floor-to-ceiling windows overlooking the lagoon and a breakfast on the balcony has never been so peaceful. The friendly staff make you feel at home and will be pleased to help you plan your time in and around Conce. Pets aren't invited to join for your stay, in order to protect the wild animals that live around here but the staff will give you the downlow on wildlife you can look out for during your stay. The lodge is on private land, so you'll need to make a reservation before driving down. Open all year. ♦$$$♦ ♦$$$$♦

a. Callejón Lagunillas 5385, Fundo Los Guindos, San Pedro de la Paz
t. +56 9 5977 7658
w. puralodge.cl

Within walking distance from Playa Larga and Playa Millaneco in Lebu, **Hosteria Millaneco** (**80**) is humble but sweet - like most of life in ocean town Lebu. The people are friendly, you can get a bite to eat and use the outdoor swimming pool, send the kids to play on the swings.. but the best thing here is the pura naturaleza. From your cabaña (4 for families, 2 for couples) you can walk straight to the beach, and, needless to say, you'll be as content as can be to enjoy a cold drink on the balcony at the end of the day. Or at any time really. Open all year. ♦$♦ ♦$$♦

a. Boca Lebu Norte, Lebu
t. +56 41 251 1540
i. hosteriamillaneco_lebu

If you followed our route to Pucón (good on ya!) you may as well follow us to **Camping Copacabana** (**81**) too. Run with love and devotion by the lovely couple Juan Carlos and Andrea, this campsite is a breath of fresh air. It's a bit of a luxury in Chile to find a place that combines peaceful camping in a natural beauty spot with clean spacious bathrooms (even wheelchair accessible) and a heated swimming pool, and compost and recycling bins, and electricity available too. Wake up to the sound of the wind in the trees and the smell of bread baking in the stone oven - Andrea bakes it fresh next to the reception each morning, nice start to the day! Pets are welcome and the campsite is open all year.
♦$♦ ♦$$♦

a. Camino a Quelhue, Pucón
t. +56 9 9249 5481
w. camping-copacabana.negocio.site

SURF

Traveling south, away from well-known spots like Puertecillo and Pichilemu, means meeting fewer surfers in the water. However, you will find a great variety of waves along the coast of Maule, Ñuble and Biobío. Expect superior lefts; especially so between Río Maule and Río Itata. Is it colder too? Yes, a little, so a wetsuit of 4mm, maybe 5mm, and warm booties will surely add to the joy of spending time in the ocean.

VICHUQUÉN (I)

Caleta Llico, north of Vichuquén, is a long black sand beach that's popular with both windsurfers and surfers of bigger boards - SUP, longboard. It's very exposed to wind but has a nice backdrop of cliffs and dunes. The old dilapidated pier may add a bit of weirdness to the scene. In a good way.

All levels/sand/shower/toilet/restaurant/surf shop/surf school/easy parking.

CONSTITUCIÓN (II)

It's highly likely that you'll find good surf along this stretch of coast. Starting at the estuary of the Maule river, a spot called **Desembocadura** delivers, depending on the sandbanks, a gentle wave. Access is easy but beware of the outgoing current. About 1 km south, at the same beach, you can check **Los Gringos** - an expert only, fast tubular wave. A challenging wave at **Piedra de la Iglesia** also demands an advanced level, especially when it's bigger than 1.5 meters. The end's pretty sketchy and very close to rocks. On smaller days, it's a fun wave for intermediate surfers. This spot requires local knowledge for safe entry and exit, and you can expect a busy beach, with an audience of sea lions watching from the rocks.

Find another consistent left at **Puerto Maguillines**, some 5 kms south of Constitución. The beautiful backdrop of hills and pine forest gives a bit of shelter from south winds.

Intermediate and advanced/sand and rocks/shower/toilet/restaurant/surf shop/surf school/easy parking.

Driving south along the M-50 towards the town of Pellines, you'll reach the wind-exposed beaches of **Caleta**

Pellines and **El Parrón**. Since these beaches are so secluded, you might want to seek local knowledge. The owner of Botilleria Punta Parrón is a local surfer who you can trust to advise accordingly.

CURANIPE (III)
♦

With a backdrop of colorful fishing boats and green hills, Caleta Curanipe offers a left pointbreak. Along the large, moon-shaped La Poza bay you'll find a few options; from **La Cruz** (close to the rocks) to the barreling **Tres Peñas** near the river mouth. Some 5 kms south from Curanipe another left called **Punta Sirena** (named after the Hotel Punta Sirena) is popular with kite and windsurfers. It works best from mid to low tide and is very exposed.

♦ *Intermediate to advanced/sand/ shower/toilet/restaurant/surf shop/surf school/easy parking.* ♦

Surrounded by a green and hilly forest, protecting it from south winds, find **Viaducto** at the bridge with the same name. You'll spot many surf stickers covering over the name on the sign. Again here, local knowledge and guidance are advised, especially since you need to find your way through the forest. Not a break for beginners. **Tregualemu** (meaning 'Forest of the Dogs' in Mapudungun) is located just over 20 kms south of Curanipe, at the Tregualemu estuary. With a medium-sized swell, if the sandbanks align, it provides lefts and rights. It also tends to draw the crowds. Get there by either hiking up a private track or paddling the length of the estuary.

COBQUECURA (IV)
♦

A long left breaks at the **Buchupureo** river, but it usually only comes to life

in winter. **La Rinconada beach**, close to Cobquecura, is a beauty of a bay, working throughout the tides. It's protected from south winds by green hills and can get kinda busy with both surfers and beachgoers. On a small swell, you can try **Monte del Zorro** beach, a few kms south. ◆ *All levels/sand and rocks/shower/toilet/restaurant/surf shop/surf school/easy parking.* ◆

CONCEPCIÓN (V)
◆

North of Concepción (or Conce as it's called by locals) find crescent-shaped white sand beach **Dichato**. A touristy place with the luxury of dressing rooms and showers, and craft stalls along its waterfront, and a perfect break for beginners. Closer to town, where the Biobío river meets the ocean, **Desembocadura** offers lefts and rights for intermediate and advanced surfers. Beware of strong currents. The spot's located within the Desembocadura Natural Park - mention that you're going surfing as you pay at the entrance and you'll get discount on your entry and parking fee. Another option suited to beginners in the Biobío region is **Las Peñas de Arauco**, an exposed beach break surrounded by stunning nature. Works best during summer, with south offshore wind and NW swell. Or try uncrowded **Playa Sector el Piure**, which works with NW wind and S to W swells.

LEBU (VI)
◆

The capital of the Arauco province, Lebu, offers options for all levels, all year round. At tranquil, southwest-facing **Playa Millaneco**, surrounded by native and pine forest, you'll find a powerful wave, beginner-friendly enough when the swell's small but

beware strong rips. At the south end of the beach, by the lighthouse and old pier, **El Faro** requires some expert skills - some sections are less demanding but it has a rocky bottom and gets busy. South of Millaneco, find **Playa Grande**, the most westerly beach in Chile. Depending on the sandbanks, there are lefts and rights to choose from that are best left to advanced level surfers. When the swell's small, find an all-level beach break at **Cuevas del Toro** (Cave of the Bull - named after the wind blowing through the cave and creating the effect of a heavy-breathing bull).

SCHOOL RENTAL SHOP

Outdoor Vichuquén (82) is a wooden shack near Llico beach. On offer are surf and windsurf lessons, rental of surf gear and fat bikes, and a shop with all the essentials. Open all year.

- **a.** J-80 981, Vichuquén
- **t.** +56 9 4204 0381
- **i.** outdoorvichuquen

Campsite, hostel and coffee bar Masi's Place also offers surf lessons and gear rental from their Escuela de Surf at **Surfcamp Maguillines (83)**. The location sits conveniently in front of a very consistent left. Owner Masi's a wealth of knowledge on the area and will happily give you some tips. Whether you're looking for good surf, a hiking trail or a restaurant - just ask Masi. Closed in winter.

- **a.** M-304, Constitución
- **t.** +56 9 7245 8526
- **i.** masis_place

Find surf and bouldering school **Punta Sureña (84)** also in Puerto Maguillines. Besides lessons you can rent all equipment. Closed in winter.

- **a.** Puerto Maguillines, Constitución
- **t.** +56 9 9837 5796
- **i.** puntasurenha

Curanipe Surf (85) offers lessons and rentals. If you want to up your game, there's individual tuition with the help of video analysis. Find them in the Curanipe beach sector, on the north side of the Pelluhue footbridge. Open all year.

- **a.** Costanera Iván Valdés S/N, Curanipe
- **t.** +56 9 8196 5127
- **w.** curanipesurf.cl

Sharing the stoke of surfing and love for the ocean with **Escuela de Surf Swell Sur (86)**, who began operating at Curanipe beach in 2008. Expect fun surf lessons from a dedicated team. Rental of boards and suits for both beginners and advanced surfers are also available. Closed in winter.

- **a.** Costanera Curanipe S/N, Curanipe
- **t.** +56 9 5114 2223
- **w.** swell-sur.webnode.cl

Waikiki Surf Shop (87) is a small surf shop but has all you may need and a bit more. Boards, wetsuits, surf accessories, and surf lessons are on offer too. The shop is run by friendly and helpful owner Pedro. Find them a short drive away from Caleta Curanipe (the main fishermen's cove) to the right of the Catholic Church. Open all year.

- **a.** Costanera Ivan Valdes S/N, Curanipe
- **t.** +56 9 8894 9591
- **fb.** Waikiki Surf Shop

Find several surf schools in Buchupureo, like **Escuela de Surf Olas Altas de Buchupureo (88)**, in Sector La Boca. Or ask for Milton from **Escuela de Surf de Buchupureo (89)**. If you're in need of a repair or looking for a handsome and crafty hand-shaped board, visit

Desastres Surfboards (90). Send him a WhatsApp message before, he might be busy in his shaping bay. Open all year.

- **a.** Buchupureo, Cobquecura
- **t.** +56 9 4970 0806
- **i.** desastresurboard

At Rinconada beach find avid surfer Nano and his enthusiastic team running **La Vieja Escuela (91)**. Surf and bodyboard lessons and rentals on the menu. Open all year.

- **a.** Playa Rinconada, Cobquecura
- **t.** +56 9 8941 1579
- **i.** escuelananosurfcobquecura

El Alto (**92**) market/surf/coffee shop is in a wooden house-style place on the road between Buchu and Cobque - you should spot the sign with a red surfboard logo in the middle of it. Get your surf essentials (sunscreen, wax, ding repair kit, spare leashes and so on) here and you can grab a coffee and some snacks to go at the same time. Open all year.

- **a.** Alto de Pullay, Cobquecura
- **i.** el_alto_pullay

Shaper/artist Benjamin Doñas makes beautiful, unique wooden boards at **Bone Fish** (**93**). All boards are 100% handmade works of art. If you think it might be a struggle to transport a life-size surfboard home but need something to remember your trip and

perfect slides by, maybe settle for a skateboard or keyring-sized board instead. Open all year.

- **a.** Las Pitras S/N, Buchupureo
- **t.** +56 9 8193 0234 / 9 8687 1737
- **i.** bonefish.wsb

In Dichato, some 36 kms north of Concepción, **Zalazar Surfboards** (**94**) offer surf lessons, rental, surf trips, and ding repairs. They've a large range of their own Zalazar boards - mainly performance shortboards and a few colorful retro fish too. Open all year.

- **a.** Avenida Daniel Vera 1292, Dichato
- **t.** +56 9 8136 1386
- **w.** zalazar.cl

French surfer and ocean-loving Jérémy Dubourg followed his heart, which led him to the Biobío coast. He set up **Escuela de Surf Rebusquedas** (**95**) and besides surf lessons, he's incredibly well informed and knows a lot about the surroundings. A go-to guy for all your need-to-knows about this stretch of coast. Find them next to Hostería Millaneco. Open all year.

- **a.** Boca Lebu Norte, Lebu
- **t.** +56 9 6831 1099
- **w.** rebusquedasurf.com

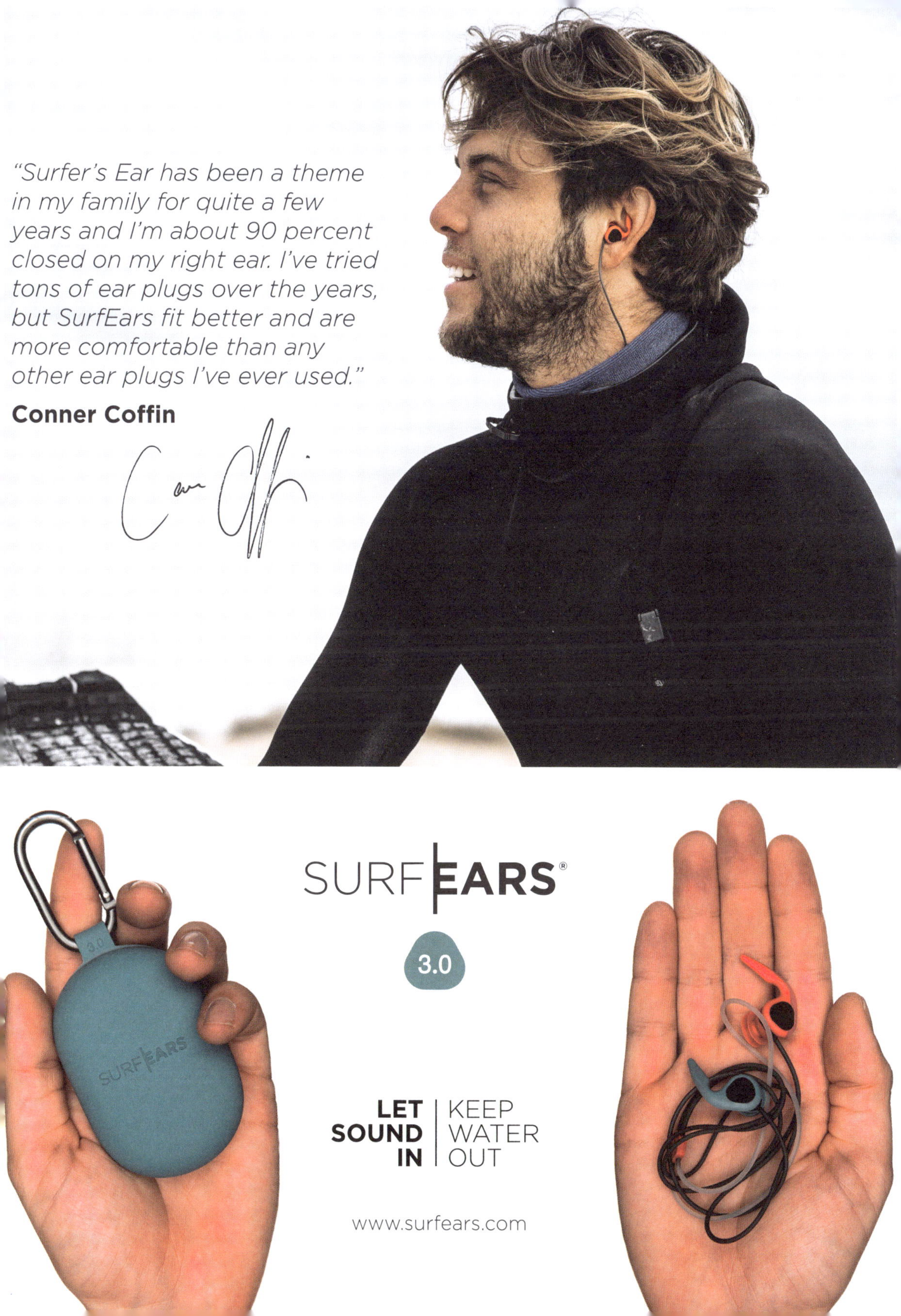

"Surfer's Ear has been a theme in my family for quite a few years and I'm about 90 percent closed on my right ear. I've tried tons of ear plugs over the years, but SurfEars fit better and are more comfortable than any other ear plugs I've ever used."

Conner Coffin

SURF EARS®

3.0

LET SOUND IN | **KEEP WATER OUT**

www.surfears.com

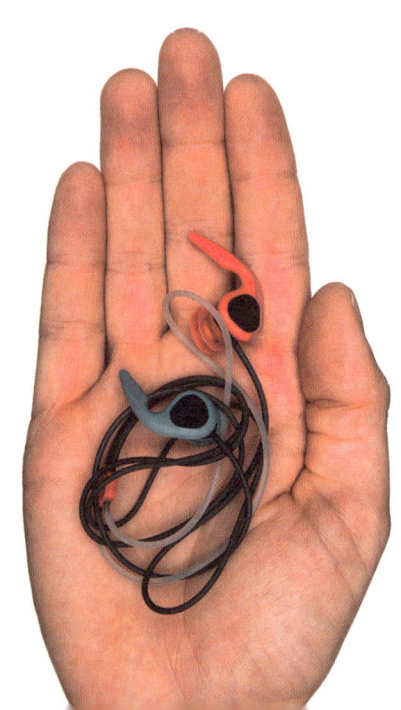

BUILDING CONFIDENCE: UTKATA KONASANA

Goddess Pose

Feel grounded and improve balance and focus with this squat variation.

Benefits:
This powerful and warming pose tones thighs and buttocks, building core strength while opening up the inner thighs and hips.

How:
Stand in a wide stance, turn your feet slightly out and squat down, but not too deep. Keep your knees in line with your toes, not rolling in or out. Imagine your legs stay open like a book, while keeping your back straight as if sliding down a wall. Keep your shoulders over your hips and open both arms so they each make an L-shape. Stay for a few breaths, relax, then repeat as many times as you like.

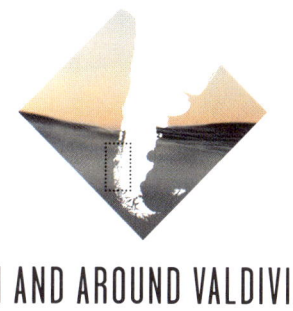

IN AND AROUND VALDIVIA

•

The capital of its province and the Región de los Ríos, the city Valdivia was once known for its shipbuilding industry and gold mining. Nowadays, the reasons you want to hang out here a while are the nature reserves, beautiful beaches and rainforest, known as Selva Valdiviana - Valdivian Jungle. And let's not forget the bustling city itself, only a 20-minute drive inland. Along the coast of the province, find top surf-stops Playa Pichicullín, Mehuín and Calfuco, and beautiful beaches like Pilolcura and Curiñanco. Pilolcura means 'hollow stone' in Mapudungun and you'll understand why - the rock formations are out-of-this-world-like, and the remote landscape gives a fallen-into-an-Avatar-movie feeling. Minus any terrifically-tall blue people, but you can use your imagination...

If you're into buzzing city vibes as a welcome change from tranquil birds and bees buzz, add Valdivia to your itinerary. The city's like a seemingly unassuming person you meet, who turns out to be the life of the party. Interesting, edgy, oddly different. The current mayor, a young woman, encourages sustainable tourism and protection of nature reserves, as well as inclusivity. You'll notice a multicultural mix, where strong influences of the Mapuche, Spanish (towers and forts), Quechua and German are present in the names of places and the styles of buildings. Once called a 'German town' owing to the influx of settlers in the 19th century, the city's known as the beer capital of Chile, with a proper Bierfest Valdivia, held in late January-early February each year. If you're not into beer, you'll find plenty options for a 'Kaffee und Kuchen'. Also a university city, Valdivia offers industrial bars full of life, students hanging out on the grass of the riverbanks, cultural events, concerts, sporting contests, and a more progressive energy than most parts of the country.

From the mesmerizing lakes of the mountains in the east, several rivers meet around the city, including the Calle-Calle, Cau-Cau and Cruces, smoothly flowing to form the Río Valdivia, which empties into Corral Bay. Here, coastal spots like Niebla (meaning fog) are steeped in history, with remnants of colonial times - from Playa Grande to the Spanish fort, Fuerte de Niebla, and Isla Mancera, which you can visit on boat tours.

Had enough of the social hubbub and longing for some slow to no internet connection and nothing-but-nature time again? Take the scenic route round to Corral (or hop over on the ferry from Niebla in an hour) and keep trucking south to explore quiet coastal hamlets and the ancient forestland of the Reserva Costera Valdiviana.

TO DO

◆

One of the familiar faces in the community of Mehuín is Geo from **Escuela de Surf NewenLafken Mehuín (1)**. Besides surf lessons (see Surf section), Geo also organizes community conservation projects such as beach cleans and other ways to protect the environment - ask him whether anything's on if you want to get involved as a volunteer while you're here. All the while you can tune up your Spanish! Open all year.

- **a.** Costanera s/n, Mehuín
- **t.** +56 9 9150 6319
- **fb.** Escuela de Surf NewenLafken Mehuín

If you fancy a change from cruising the coastline, a couple of hours' drive inland, close to the Argentinian border, **Huilo-Huilo Biological Reserve (2)** offers a multitude of mountain activities. The drive from the west takes you along 30 kms of the jaw-droppingly gorgeous Panguipulli Lake. The nearest town is Neltume, and while you'll find the surroundings can get crowded in high season, the set-up of the reserve, its well-protected and well-preserved nature, and its stunning facilities invite you to dive into nature way away from any thronging. However, it's still a smart idea to book ahead, no matter when you decide to go. Activities on offer range from a number of walking trails and treks to a bike park and pump track, or hot springs boat tours - across the majestic lake to a secluded hot spring in the middle of the forest, where you can drift away in a private thermal bath cut out of a hollow tree. Also on the activity menu: sunset picnic tours to the Mocho-Chonshuesco Volcano, a visit to Darwin's Frog Dissemination Center, wild boar watching, deer watching, kayaking, river rafting, craft workshops, a volcano museum, ski, snowboard and snowmobile opportunities galore or (the adrenaline-boost option) flying through the tree canopies on zip lines - they've a dedicated children's canopy too! If you want to do them all, you'd best check out the accommodation offerings, ranging from camping to luxury hotels, see Sleep Section. Open all year.

- **a.** Carretera Internacional CH-203, Km 55, Neltume
- **t.** +56 2 2887 3510
- **w.** huilohuilo.com

Hike in the Selva Valdiviana, where you'll find various easy trails with astonishing views in **Parque Oncol** (**3**). Within a couple of hours you can make it to the top of this private protected wilderness park, located in the Cordillera de la Costa. If the fog allows, you'll be able to see the sea, the city and some volcanoes that can be spotted from the peak. Dogs are not allowed, in order to protect the native flora and fauna. Open all year.

a. Oncol Park, Los Laureles 222
t. +56 800 370 222
w. parqueoncol.cl

Reserva Punta Curiñanco (**4**) offers another beautiful hiking opportunity, along a 3-kilometer track that leads through a luscious little rainforest to several miradores - ocean viewpoints - and eventually to the beach. The paths are well kept by the caretakers, who charge a fair entrance fee and will give you advice on what to look out for where. Open all year.

a. Curiñanco
t. +56 9 8335 5938

See the city from the water with **SUP Valdivia Travesías** (**5**). Local waterwoman Fran doesn't just rent out boards but takes guided tours (in Spanish, English or French) customized to your wishes. Nothing standard and touristy, but a super professional and chill vibe, and such a great experience. She also offers an epic full moon tour which includes refreshments - local beers and kombucha. Fran's a surf photographer too, so look out for her on the beach when you're practicing your hang tens, floaters, 360s and whatnots. Open all year.

a. General Lagos 1445, Valdivia
t. +56 9 8345 4980
fb. SUP Valdivia Travesías

Immerse yourself in a wide range of contemporary art at the newly renovated **Museo de Arte Contemporáneo de Valdivia** (**6**). Settled pretty much in front of the Feria Fluvial, but on the other side of the river, so once your cultural needs are satisfied, you can enjoy the view over the river and city center from the museum. Open all year.

a. Avenida Los Laureles s/n, Isla Teja, Valdivia
t. +56 63 222 1968
w. macvaldivia.cl

Cross the Pedro Valdivia Bridge on foot (**7**) to get a whole different energy from when you drive over it. From the bridge you'll have an iconic picture-postcard view of the city and tourist boats along the Schuster Pier. Besides a nice view, this bridge has big history - it's survived numerous natural disasters, including floods and the largest earthquake recorded in human history (1960 Valdivia Earthquake), while most nearby buildings were destroyed. So, you can be pretty sure that it's safe to cross back and forth as many times as you like!

a. Puente Pedro de Valdivia, Valdivia

Visit the Spanish fort and national monument Fuerte de Niebla, managed by the **Museo de Sitio Castillo de Niebla** (**8**) where 'the walls tell the story', to learn some about the history of this area. And the neighboring lighthouse for a pretty picture - cos everyone loves a lighthouse. Open all year from Tuesday to Saturday, free entry but you'll need to register online to book a visit time and show ID on arrival.

a. Del Castillo, Niebla
t. +56 63 233 6182
w. museodeniebla.gob.cl

EAT/DRINK/HANG OUT

◆

As you drive along Playa Mehuín, you'll find the little wooden kiosk of **La Bary Brunch** (**9**). Friendly place that offers tostas, snacks, coffees and juices and a view over the beach. Open from December to February only. ◆$◆

a. Los Choros, Mehuín
t. +56 9 6453 4944
fb. La Bary Brunch

For a good selection of beers and pretty decent food too, **La Ultima Frontera** (**10**) should do the job. It's always busy, filled with great vibes and color, and reasonably priced. This popular café-restaurant-bar serves everything from sandwiches and snacks to burgers and traditional food, and drinks - fresh fruit juices and veggie options are also on offer if you want something lighter - for brunch, lunch or dinner. Open from December to January, closed on Sundays. ◆$◆ ◆$$◆

a. Vicente Pérez Rosales 787, Valdivia
t. +56 63 223 5363
w. laultimafrontera.cl

Located on Isla Teja, you'll find hip brewery/bar **El Growler** (**11**) with a garden full of sturdy wooden tables. They've every drink you can think of on their list and make a mean homemade kombucha - that'll help you through last night's local craft beer tasting and have you ready to start again! The food's good and they've a varied menu, from bar snacks, salads and falafels to tacos and burgers, but it's a popular place so be prepared to wait a while on the weekend. Open all year. ◆$$◆

a. Saelzer 41, Isla Teja, Valdivia
t. +56 63 222 9545
w. elgrowler.cl

Families and pets alike will get a warm reception at **La Tribu** (**12**) where they've not only a secure play area for little humans, but an inclusive toilet too - way to welcome the whole tribe together! The space is very light, with a hipster vibe, and beautiful photos of people all around the world hang on the walls. It's a favorite place for brunch or lunch and offers lots of healthy options and a children's menu alongside good portions for big people, tasty sweet bites, fresh juices and specialty coffees. Open all year. ◆$$◆

a. Saelzer 71, Isla Teja, Valdivia
t. +56 63 220 8711
w. latribuvaldivia.cl

Cafe Cotidiano (13) is a cozy coffee place in the city center. On weekdays, a steady stream of students and people on their way to work stop in for their daily brew-to-go. Our favorites here are their French crêpes and croissants, a welcoming variant to the usual pan con palta (avo on toast), and asking for plant-based milk in your coffee isn't frowned upon. Open all year. ◆$◆ ◆$$◆

a. Arauco 280, Valdivia
t. +56 63 220 0697
i. valdiviacotidiano

Ubuntu (14) is one of the places that you need to know about (you're welcome) as it's 'hidden' inside a house. Walk in the front door and out to a big sunny garden full of tables, hangout spots and colorful lights. Besides being a 100% vegan restaurant where almost all is homemade, Ubuntu is so much more than that - hence its tagline, 'Lugar del Encuentro' (meeting spot). Owner Marybel wanted to create an inclusive place where all people can meet, feel safe, and be themselves without feeling judged by the crowd. This is why she didn't pick a typical restaurant setting but went for a house instead. Less formal, easier to connect and exchange ideas, hang out with your pet, meet other travelers, and perhaps talk to someone with a different background to yours. The name Ubuntu was chosen very intentionally - it's a term that originates in Africa and freely translates to 'exchanging and building together'. It's easy to say that Marybel has succeeded in turning her ideas into reality and created a unique and special place in the city, which you'll likely want to return to. Seasonal opening varies, best check online or give them a call. ◆$$◆

a. O'Higgins 210, Valdivia
t. +56 9 7814 0386
i. ubuntuvaldivia.cl

For yet more proof that plant-based food's got plenty flavor and style, stop by at **Sabor a Verde (15)**. Their cakes and pastries look like pieces of art - almost too pretty to eat. Once you do, though, you'll probably want to order more. The owners are friendly chatty folk and run their 100% plant-based business with zest and love. Grab some tasty treats and/or stuffed-with-superfoods sandwiches to start your day full of adventures with a zing. Open all year, closed in the evenings. ◆$◆ ◆$$◆

a. Camilo Henríquez 822, Valdivia
t. +56 9 5233 5148
i. sabor.a.verde

Café Cosas Ricas (16) is a locally well-known restaurant-slash-coffee-place-slash-bar, all in one, depending on what time of the day you wander in. Although spacious, a homely atmosphere has been created by making great use of lighting, stylish vintage furniture, plants, art and antique knick-knacks. Good food, a large selection of cake and specialty coffees, and pretty fast wifi (not always a given in these parts) make this place ever so easy to recommend. Open all year. ◆$$◆

a. Pérez Rosales 644, Valdivia
t. +56 63 222 0606
i. cosasricas.valdivia

Café la Motoneta (17) takes 'quirky' to the next level. The roadside café makes a fun stop, offering a Peruvian menu with a good variety on the menu and a very varied décor to admire. The walls and ceiling are decorated with odd memorabilia: road signs, t-shirts, photos and all sorts of objects. Open all year. ◆$◆

a. Del Castillo 995, Niebla
t. +56 63 227 2030
fb. cafe la motoneta

SHOP

The lively riverside market, **Feria Fluvial (18)** (River Fair), is one of the city's main tourist attractions and a colorful reminder of Valdivia's ancient trade history. Held on the eastern bank of Río Valdivia, by the Schuster pier, with stalls offering fish, meat,

local produce, handmade crafts and souvenirs. The smells, sounds and bustling crowd create a long stretch of entertaining chaos, typical of a South American marketplace. And you'll spot sea lions lounging along the waterfront towards La Costanera, wise to the easy spoils on offer as tourists and fishmongers throw them scraps. (Of course, if you've any knowledge about the taboos of feeding wild animals, you'll know this shouldn't really be encouraged.) Open daily, all year round.

a. Libertad 28, Valdivia

At **Majen (19)** they sell ethically made beauty products, containing all the secret skin wonders that the ancient Valdivian forest has to offer. All products are cruelty free, come in beautiful packaging, and feel like bottles filled with the best of Southern Chile. Next to all the daily essentials you might need, they have specialized products like massage oils for pregnant ladies and babies, and even a line of products for men. Stop by to stock up on the best of local oils and creams. Open all year.

a. Esmeralda 695, Valdivia
t. +56 63 220 7214
w. majen.cl

Sensorial (20) will certainly satisfy your sense of smell, the moment you walk in the door. If the wafting scents from the walls full of tea don't make you want to buy one of each, ask the friendly staff what they recommend. With everything from pure tea plant 'tés' to infusiones and blends, coffees and chocolates. Here's also a good place to pick up some classic Yerba Maté and the kit you'll need to drink it the way South Americans do. The well-known energizing tea is Argentina's national drink and it's a longstanding tradition to take a maté with friends and/or family - to partake properly you'll need a cuia (special maté mug) and a bomba (special maté metal straw). Open all year.

a. Pérez Rosales 681, Valdivia
t. +56 63 225 2035
w. sensorial.cl

SLEEP
◆

Camping y Cabañas Mi Paraíso Natural (21) is off the road just outside of Mehuín, and the loveliest camping spot in the area. Just like most of Mehuín, facilities here are humble but nature definitely isn't! Lots of green, flowers, plants, and the sound of the river running alongside, envelop you once you set foot in this natural paradise. As this camping is small - basically the beautiful hidden garden of a very friendly local who lives in the house at the entrance - it's not suitable for vans. If you want to stay but don't have a tent, you can leave your van at the entrance and rent a simple cabin. Closed in winter. Off season you can call owners Alicia and Luiz, if they're around they might be able to make an arrangement for you.

a. Hijuela n2, Camino a Queule, Mehuín
t. +56 9 8902 6579
i. miparaisonaturalmehuin

A very basic option (even for Mehuín standards), but right in front of the beach and perfectly flat for vans to park up, is **Camping Rewe Lafken Mehuin (22)**. They charge per hour and per site (not per person), so you can stop in for the day/afternoon only, and park up to set up your sunscreen and prep some food for a few hours. Facilities are very basic: a simple bathroom, picnic table and bench, and a place for a fire. If you're content with simple pleasures, like being straight across the street from the beach, it'll suit you just fine. Seasonal opening. ◆$◆

a. T-270, Mehuín

Pilolcura Lodge (23) is the only accommodation in this tiny pueblo right in front of Playa Pilolcura. The lodge consists of just five very cozy and nicely decorated rooms, which have

a spacious and light set-up. The balconies might be even bigger than the rooms themselves and are perfect for a siesta in your hammock with the sound of the ocean to soothe you. At night you can have a beer or put some food on the BBQ on the shared patio (there aren't any restaurants nearby so bring some groceries) with a magical stargazing experience for entertainment - there's no light pollution in this remote place. Breakfast is simple, and wifi hasn't made it to Pilolcura yet. Cows, however, have - you'll see them strolling on the beach in between the people. Truly a special place. Open all year. ◆$$$◆

a. Playa Pilolcura, Pilolcura
t. +56 9 6472 9876
i. pilolcuralodge

Our absolute favorite spot to stay in the city is **Hotel Nueve Rios (24)**, named after the Mapudungun name for Valdivia. The hotel opened in 2018 and used to be an original German-style house. Once owner Nicolas removed the old wallpaper he discovered beautiful wooden walls, which he decided to keep and make a feature of. This resulted in a very cozy space with a laid-back, bed and breakfast kind of vibe. You'll feel far more at home than in a hotel, yet with great bathroom facilities, a very comfy mattress and everything spick and span. Located a short walk from the main sights Valdivia has to offer, it's the perfect base for a few days exploring the city. Make sure to book in advance, as many travelers know about this little golden nugget. Open all year. ◆$$◆ ◆$$$◆

a. Carlos Anwandter 629, Valdivia
t. +56 9 9224 5913
w. hotelnueverios.cl

Camping Familiar Agua de la Piedra (25) is situated in the forest in between the city and Niebla. This pet-friendly campsite with a little stream running through the trees is a super spot to disconnect and immerse yourself in nature. They've friendly pricing, hot water and clean bathrooms, and also comfortable little wooden cabañas con hot tubs and woodburners to rent. What else could you need? Open from October to April, the cabañas are available all year. ◆$◆

a. Agua del Obispo km 12, Camino a Niebla, Valdivia
t. +56 9 8555 7946
fb. Camping Agua de la Piedra

Cabañas Fischer (26) offer cabins built on the cliffs of Niebla's coast, each cabin with a private terrace - all overlooking the cliffs and the ocean. Run by the Fischer family, fun and friendly people who have poured oodles of love into their cabins and flourishing garden, just a 5-minute walk from the beach. It's a stay where you

can relax and recharge, feel right at home and warmly welcomed, but also have privacy and wifi. Several cabins vary in size, from sleeping 2 people to supersize family cabins with hot tubs. All are built with wood and natural elements to blend in with the surroundings and are decorated beautifully. No pets allowed, open all year. ♦$$♦ ♦$$$♦

a. Del Castillo 1119, Niebla
t. +56 9 7695 6725
w. cabanasfischer.net

Located right at the entrance to the town of Niebla is **Cabañas y Camping Santa Clara (27)**. A quiet, green, and easy-going campsite with its own path down to the beach. It never gets boring to brush your teeth in the morning while one of the sheep that live on the campsite slowly walks by and stops to stare at you before continuing their morning stroll. There are sunny and shaded spots to choose from, a swimming pool, a swing for kids, and clean facilities. Cabins are also available for rent and you'll likely meet some returning guests - always a good sign! Pet friendly and good wifi. Open all year. ♦$♦

a. Cochrane 855, Niebla
t. +56 9 7944 7262
w. cabanas-y-camping-santa-clara.negocio.site

Already mentioned in the To Do section for its huge choice of activities, the **Huilo-Huilo Biological Reserve (28)** is a couple of hours' drive inland and has almost as many accommodation options as activities. Located in the middle of the native forest, at Camping Huilo-Huilo they've lots of spots suitable for small to mid-size tents, and a few options for bigger tents and campervans/motorhomes. The site's the type where people are quiet and respectful of nature, turning in early and rising early for a sunrise hike. Electricity is available, most spots have their own picnic bench, and showers/toilets are clean. If you're after a superior lodging option you can choose from big or small cabins, the backpackers hostel, the canopy village, or one of the hotels - the most remarkable being the fairytale-like Hotel Nothofagus, where the style and design will fill you with wonder. All options put you in a beautiful and inspired space which will connect you with the magic of Huilo-Huilo's nature. Make sure to book in advance. Open all year. ♦$$$♦ ♦$$$$♦

a. Carretera Internacional CH-203, km 60, Neltume
t. +56 9 4789 5946
w. huilohuilo.com

IN AND AROUND PUCATRIHUE

•

The area around San Juan de la Costa's all about simple pleasures and exploring, luscious green sweeps of forest and stunning white sand beaches. While the main three settlements, Pucatrihue, Bahía Mansa, and Maicolpué, are only a few kilometers apart, other coastal spots you might want to check out are remote and secluded, almost to the point of isolation, so don't expect to find a coast road connecting them all. More likely you'll need to take a boat trip or hike a few hours to find the hidden treasures. A sturdy vehicle will serve you well for bumpy rides, and you'll find the lack of tourism and development as refreshing as the cool ocean temperature. The Huilliche-Mapuche, indigenous people from these parts - Huilliche meaning People from the South - are a warm and friendly community with their roots deep in the native culture and traditions of their ancestors.

Here's the place to take crazyscapes into nature, trust the locals rather than online maps, throw some essentials (water, snacks, cash, a bag to take away any trash) in a rucksack and go and explore. From deserted bays like Caleta Manzano to the mountain ranges of Choroy Traiguén, swim in the lagoon at Playa Tril Tril, trek through untouched forest in the Mapu Lahual Park Network. As for waves, the fishing village Pucatrihue (commonly referred to as Puca) is your best option and has pretty much nada going on in the way of surf tourism. Yet. We're not sure we'll be able to say the same in a few years though. What we can be fairly certain of, is that the sacred rock Abuelito Huenteao (Grandfather Huenteao) will still be settled on the sanctuary rocks in the bay, spreading his protection to those in need. According to Huilliche mythology, he mediates between the Huilliche people and their divinities, and helps his people with their living conditions, fishing, crops, weather and such. It's also possible that he owns or has the power of the sea, so you might want to pay your respects to him while you're here.

TO DO

♦

Take the curvy road up from the playa of Pucatrihue to **Mirador Choroy Traiguen (29)** to get a bananas-panorama from the viewpoint; the combo of blue pacific, green forest, mountainous backdrop and the mouth of Río Llesquehue makes a marvel of a feast for the eyes (and insta shots). Accessible all year.

a. Mirador Choroy Traiguen, Pucatrihue

Go freestyle and hop onto one of the **boat tour options from Bahía Mansa (30)**. There's little in the way of websites or advance bookings for these excursions, so whether you're

hoping to see penguins or whales or to heave-ho (it could be a bumpy ride) all the way to a remote playa down the coast, you'll find some adventure or other to sail to from this picturesque little fishing cove. While you're waiting you might find yourself following your nose to a selection of stalls selling fresh tasty seafood marinadas and empanadas along the beachfront. Accessible all year, tours dependent on weather/sea conditions.

a. Bahía Mansa

The enchanting cove of **Caleta Cóndor (31)** is where you'll really feel the magic of the land. This beautiful remote settlement at the mouth of Río Cholguaco is inhabited by a handful

of indigenous families who provide basic camping and cabins, along with one beach restaurant (Alerce Food, see Eat section) and a mini-mercado. Alongside the beach a small island, named 'Isla Tortuga' for its turtle shape, creates shelter for a stunning lagoon. The green water of the lagoon next to the pacific blue shallow bay and jungle backdrop makes for the biggest and best get away from the real world vibes you can imagine. The first people that settled here made their living from the wood of the native Alerce trees - slow-growing cypress trees - you'll see the odd wood carving or sign made from it, along with stone stacks and an occasional fence or bit of decking, otherwise the landscape's as natural as can be. Hike along

endless trails, take the path from behind the restaurant to a mighty fine viewpoint (approx. an hour with a winding climb) where you pay a small entrance fee to enter the property of a welcoming local and enjoy the vista. The easiest way to get here is on a 2-3 hour (depending on sea conditions) boat trip from Bahía Mansa. (NB the boats only sail in summer, they are small so if the sea's choppy you might want to skip brrreakfaaaast.) If you're put off by fear of sea sickness and have a good sense of adventure and level of fitness, you can make it on a hike (allow a full day and pack for a wilderness adventure with plenty of water, snacks, cash) through the Mapu Lahual Park Network.

You can start from nearby locations Caleta Huellelhue (Playa Rano) or Playa Tril Tril, depending on how fit you're feeling. The hike crosses a number of sections that include beaches, barras and an estuary, which require little boat rides, so we recommend you use a local tour guide. Wifi's not something you're going to come upon and there's no tour operator offering advance bookings for these trips but you might get a phone signal in places and we can recommend a few useful contacts. Failing those, Alonso Hinostroza of Altos de Pichi Mallay Lodge in Maicolpué is kind of the unofficial tourist ambassador of the area: book a stay at his place and you'll get all the up-to-date contact info and travel advice you could dream of. Check Sleep section for places to stay. Accessible all year.

a. Caleta Cóndor
t. +56 9 7209 3249 / 9 5713 5690
i. caletacondorrutamilenaria / turismo_riosur

EAT/DRINK/HANG OUT

Family-owned restaurant **Quincho La Cascada del Chucao** (32) is well known locally for their award-winning fried empanadas and is perched on the hilltop above Pucatrihue, with a stunning view out to the horizon from the wooden terrace. Also serving seafood and ceviche, they've a beautiful wall of art representing local heritage and their own cascada (waterfall) view too. A steep path leads down from the parking area to the waterfall if you want to walk your meal off after dining, or wander down beforehand to work up a good appetite. Open all year for lunch or early dinner, from March to December only weekends and

holidays. ◆$$◆

a. Choroy Traiguén, Pucatrihue
t. +56 9 9528 5264
fb. Quincho Cascada del Chucao

Driving out of Bahía Mansa on the U-40, at the turning left towards Contaco and Pucatrihue you´ll see one of the Escultura Madera series - wooden sculptures representing the Huilliche culture which are dotted around the area - this one's a lady working on a loom. Almost directly behind in the house on your right, find **Tortillas al Rescoldo (33)** in the home of Maria Pilar. Prepared in traditional style, using the recipe handed down through her family, Maria bakes her tortillas in a self-built outdoor 'sand' oven. Best eaten warm,

straight from the oven, with some cheese or some of Maria's home-made marmalade but of course if you can resist, save them for your picnic later. Open all year, from March to December only weekends and holidays. ◆$◆

a. U-40/U-300 Junction, Bahía Mansa

Hosteria La Casa del Mar (34) is owned by Cristina, who knows how to cook and does it with her heart and soul, then adds a pinch of joy on top. You may well hear her warm laugh coming from the kitchen as you sit on the terrace overlooking the bay. Cristina uses local seasonal products and is all about celebrating Ñuke Mapu (Mother Earth) and the flavors and aromas of her ancestral culture in her kitchen - so you can expect just-landed fish and shellfish, locally reared meat, native fruits and organic veggies, freshly baked breads and droolworthy desserts, all prepared with love and beautifully presented too. We expect you'll want to stay forever, and you can! See Sleep section for accommodation info. Open all year, off season it's recommended to call ahead. ◆$$◆

a. Bahía Mansa 289
t. +56 9 9214 3774
w. hosterialacasadelmar.com

Find lots of seafood, meat and salads on the menu at **Restaurant Raíces de Pichi Mallay (35)** and a pretend you're on a big ol' sailboat set-up on

their terrace. High up on the hill to the south of Maicolpué, the wooden decking's been created to make you feel like you're dining on a boat in the sky. No sealegs required, no wobbling or waves up here. A lovely spot for lunch on a sunny day. Open all year, best to call and make a reservation as seasonal opening times vary. ◆ $ $ ◆

a. Maicolpué Río Sur
t. +56 9 4773 3795
i. raices_pichimallay

Alerce Food (**36**) is the only restaurant you'll find on Caleta Cóndor and is located right on the beach. Run by a friendly local family who serve simple dishes like salads, fries and the fresh catch of the day. Nothing fancy, but just fine. They also have a mini market where you can buy basic provisions - handy if you're planning to camp and stay a while. Don't forget to bring cash. Open from December to March. ◆$◆

a. Caleta Cóndor

SLEEP

Hosteria La Casa del Mar (**37**) sits sweetly on the hill above Bahía Mansa, offering a simple homely comfortable stay and astounding views from the rooms overlooking the ocean (tip: request the ocean view when you make your booking). Run by local Cristina and her family along with the help of some four-legged family members, the ground floor serves as a living room/restaurant area (see Eat section), and bedrooms on the second floor are varying sizes for couples or solo travelers. One bathroom is shared between guests, as is the wooden hot tub in the garden. You'll be very content here if you're on a budget and/or happy with a basic stay and cheerful company. Open all year. ◆$◆

a. Bahía Mansa 289
t. +56 9 9214 3774
w. hosterialacasadelmar.com

Sleeping with the sound of the waves as your background track is reality at **Hosteria Miller** (**38**). Right in front of Maicolpué beach, the red wooden house has simple bedrooms, a shared bathroom and a restobar, as well as a bunch of hammocks in the front yard ready to welcome you. Open all year. ◆$$◆

a. Maicolpué
fb. Hosteria Miller

Altos de Pichi Mallay Lodge (**39**) is your best bet for a room or camping spot in the area. Getting there can be tricky as the road isn't in great condition - find it by going uphill from Maicolpué and looking for the sign to the right which points to the lodge. Follow this road to the wooden fence, enter through the gate and continue until you see the big wooden house pop up ahead of you. The land, a tranquil piece of paradise where it's easy to disconnect, belongs to Alonso Hinostroza and his family. Alonso's dad built the lodge himself - a big bright home with a large sun deck, hammocks and hot tub spots, cozy rooms and shared bathrooms. On the inside, mamá's in charge - keeping all rooms squeaky clean and filling the air with the smell of cakes for breakfast each morning. It's easy to feel at home in this spacious place with plenty of natural light,. The camping is located next to the lodge, with a green field and native forest. Some incredible viewpoints look out over the ocean from a great height (yoga heaven!) and hiking trails have been created around the land for guests to enjoy peaceful nature at its purest. Open all year. ◆$◆ ◆$$◆

a. Rio Sur Camino a Tril Tril, Maicolpué
t. +56 9 8447 7304
fb. Altos de Pichi Mallay Lodge

Camping Las Cascadas De Caleta Cóndor (**40**) is one of the handful of camping grounds in this magical back to-basics destination. Try to choose a grassy spot for your tent from which you can see the horses grazing contentedly as you build your campfire, prepare to cook your food wild-style and gaze at the night sky. Buenas noches. Open all year (but be aware boats only run in high season, off season you need to hike). ◆$◆

a. Caleta Cóndor
t. +56 9 8484 6400
fb. Camping Las Cascadas De Caleta Condor

IN AND AROUND ISLA GRANDE DE CHILOÉ

Following Ruta 5 - the Pan-American Highway - to Pargua, you're nearing Northern Patagonia, and the end of this book. From here a ferry crosses the Chacao channel to Chiloé Island. Before hopping on the half hour ferry ride, however, you might want to explore the Llanquihue area a little. The colorful town of Puerto Varas may be on your itinerary, with its German influences and even their own Oktoberfest and Kuchen. It's an outdoor lover's idea of heaven - situated on the south end of Lago Llanquihue, surrounded by national parks, volcanoes, mountains and green valleys. Or find secluded beaches between Maullín and Carelmapu.

Once you set foot on Chiloé there's no escaping the color green. With generous rainfall throughout the year, find green hills dotted with sheep and sometimes feral Chilote ponies, impenetrable forests and mountain ranges. Along its quieter waterways, lakes and rivers, the cheerfully colored palafitos - traditional wooden houses on stilts - brighten up even the cloudiest of days. Although wearing your swimsuit here is a bit of a stretch, given that the climate isn't the warmest, even in summer, it's quite a contrast spotting the snowy mountain tops of mainland Patagonia from the east side of the island on a warm sunny day.

Isla Grande de Chiloé is the largest of the archipelago of over 30 islands, and short ferry rides make island-hopping ever so easy. The island itself is just under 200 kms long and 60 kms wide but has picturesque beaches aplenty - like the sandy stretch at the Duhatao rivermouth where forest meets ocean. This beach even has its own (basic) campsite and cabins. As for surfing; the islanders, Chilotes, have a strong connection to the ocean but riding waves is of more recent years. Your best chance of finding rideable waves is around Faro Corona. But having said that, respecting the delicate line between an undisclosed paradise and prospects of exploring the unknown, we strongly advise that you connect with local surfers before setting out on your own search.

Although you've reached the final chapter of this book, you're far from the southernmost part of Chile. If you're journeying further south you'll be heading on a whole new adventure, without us; these parts deserve their own guidebook and ours ends with chapter Chiloé. You'll no doubt want to do thorough research before trucking on to the icy landscape of South Patagonia. If you want to skip the first leg of the journey, rather than ferrying back to Pargua and driving the 1240 km-long highway (Carretera Austral, Ruta 7) between Puerto Montt and Villa O'Higgins, you can sail from one of the island's harbors, Quellón or Castro, to Chaitén. (Check the ferry schedule in advance, especially in summer, it's a 4 to 6 hour crossing). You'll be missing out on a beautiful route though. We wish you safe travels from here!

TO DO

♦

You'll find most folk exploring the Los Lagos region tend to skip the town of **Carelmapu (41)**, and head straight to Chiloé Island. But surfing and beaching wise you're likely to enjoy the remote playas. Named Carelmapu, meaning 'green land' in Mapudungun, for obvious reasons, the fishing village may be small and unassuming, the surroundings, however, are lush. Any outdoor lover will appreciate the simple pleasures of staying, hiking, or wandering about vast forests and along clifftops. Driving from Carelmapu towards the tip of the peninsula you'll spot the Church of Carelmapu, built in 1913. This picturesque wooden church hosts one of the oldest religious celebrations in southern Chile - the fiesta of Virgen de Candelaria - honoring the patron saint of fishermen, dating as far back as the early 17th century. Each year in February, the fishermen carry Nuestra Señora de la Candelaria on a platform from the church to the sea, where hundreds of people meet at the shoreline to honor her. Although the island's surrounded by it, the ocean was long considered a dangerous place because of the many fishermen who have lost their lives at sea. Arturo, the owner of Carelmapu Surf Camp, takes pride in taking local children surfing and teaching them awareness about the ocean. With more and more traveling surfers arriving, and locals getting a taste for it too, the attitude towards the ocean's slowly changing. Playa Mar Brava, some 4 kms out of town, ticks many boxes of a surfer's fancy: plenty room to roam, wild and stunning scenery of trees bordering the beach, cliffs to the south and endless black sand beach and green hills to the north. You can drive to the beach and, since there are no facilities, make sure to take all your trash, leaving no trace of your visit.

Knowledgeable local guide César from **Viajante Verde (42)** takes you on outdoor adventures around the Maullín and Carelmapu area. Whether you choose a kayak trip along the wetlands, hike, or excursion to the geological formations on the Amortajado Peninsula, he'll happily lead the way and share his expertise. Available all year.

a. María Luisa Bombal 519, Maullín
t. +56 9 7954 2099
i. verdeviajante

One of the reasons many visit the Chiloé archipelago is to observe penguins and sea birds, while also hoping to see whales pass by. **Ecoturismo Puñihuil (43)** offer boat tours around the 3 islets of Puñihuil. Find locals such as a mixed colony of Humboldt and Magellan penguins, sea otters and sea lions hanging out, and then there's a good chance of spotting blue or humpback whales and dolphins. The tours are popular but limited to a few a day - and rightfully so, to minimize disturbance and protect the valuable marine eco system - so it's advisable to book in advance. Tours are available from September to March.

a. Puñihuil, Chiloé
t. +56 9 8317 4302
w. pinguineraschiloe.cl

Along the inlets, lakes and canals of the island you'll see the iconic **Palafitos (44)**. Although many of the 19th-century stilt houses were destroyed by earthquakes and/or floods, you can still see a good number of them, especially in the Gamboa neighborhood on the outskirts of Castro. Originally constructed by fishing families, who could hop into their boats directly from the house, these days they're divided between those still used as homes for islanders and fishermen and those converted into restaurants or small hotels.

a. Castro, Chiloé

The wooden churches of Chiloé are as iconic as the palafitos. Built entirely from native wood and constructed without the use of nails but rather wooden joints, using the exceptional expertise of local carpenters and boat builders. Some of the island's churches are listed World Heritage by UNESCO because of their unique use of both European and indigenous architecture, blending into the surroundings and serving the community. Most are built on hills, so sailors and fishermen could see them while out at sea and use them as orientation points. While in Castro, you might want to visit the **Iglesia de San Francisco (45)**, located in the city's main square - Plaza de Armas. Although built in a slightly different style, Neo-Gothic, it's by far the largest. Open all year.

a. Carretera Panamericana Sur 462, Castro, Chiloé

The **Chiloé National Park (46)** holds several hiking options. The park, an area of over 400 square kms on the west coast of the island, includes dunes, dense rainforest, swamps and bogs. But most is taken up by the mountains of the Chilean Coastal Range. There are short loop trails and easy walks using wooden walkways, but also longer treks like the Huentemó Cole Cole trail that runs along the coast and passes Cole Cole beach (where sometimes you can see wild horses roaming). You can camp in certain areas for a small fee, paid to the indigenous community. The easiest way to access is by the entrance at Cucao and Muelle de las Almas. Open all year.

a. Parque Nacional Chiloé, Chiloé
t. +56 65 253 2501
w. conaf.cl/parques/parque-nacional-chiloe/

Hike along Punta Pirulil and up to **Muelle de Las Almas (47)**, the dock or pier of souls. The wooden pier is an art installation by Chilean wood sculptor Marcelo Orellana Rivera. It depicts a carrier of souls of the dead over the sea into the afterlife, inspired by a Mapuche story. It's incredible scenery overlooking the ocean and high cliffs. The beauty also lies in the journey, walking across the green hills, maybe greeting a few cows or wild horses. The hike from the car park to the pier takes about an hour and we recommend going early morning if you want to avoid having too many fellow visitors in your way. To get to the car park in the forest, from which you can hike to the pier: in Cucao follow the W-848 towards Rahue. The owners of the land ask a small entrance fee, cash only. Open all year, but the best time to visit's during the summer.

a. Punta Pirulil, Cucao, Chiloé
fb. Muelle de las Almas

EAT/DRINK/HANG OUT

◆

Pizza Brava (48) offers homemade thin crust pizzas with add-on options such as fresh local cheese, along with surf vibes and chill-a-lot music. The restaurant's run by friendly local surfer Camilo and his partner so you may get some tips for nearby beaches with your order. Located along the main street that forms the heart of this tiny town. Open in summer. ◆$◆

a. Circunvalación, Carelmapu
t. +56 9 7579 2235
i. pizzabravacarelmapu

Cafetería La Ola (49) makes for a lovely morning stop before heading to the beach. Its bright blue colors are

as fresh as their brews and pastries. They've some handmade arts and crafts for sale too. Open all year. ◆$◆

a. Calle O'Higgins, Carelmapu
t. +56 9 7646 6234
i. cafeteria_laola

Café Blanco (50) serves great coffee, delicious pastries, cakes and ice creams, and they're okay with you using their wifi to tick some off your digital to do list. They also sell some (tasteful!) souvenirs in the little shop section at the back. Open all year. ◆$◆ ◆$$◆

a. Eleuterio Ramirez 359, Ancud, Chiloé
t. +56 65 262 0197
i. cafeblancoancud

Restaurante Quetalmahue (51) is one of the few restaurants who prepare Curanto - a local Chilote dish - in the traditional way. Curanto's also eaten in southern parts of Chile and Argentina but originated in Chiloé. Usually containing portions of seafood, meat, vegetables and potatoes, the preparation is quite a sight; heated rocks are used to line a cooking pit in the ground, then the ingredients are layered, each layer separated by leaves (cabbage, fig or rhubarb). All is topped with earth and then left to cook for some hours. To watch the prep rather than just rock up and eat it (ha - see what we did there) it's best to check their prep-plus-serving times and make a reservation. Find them some 15 kms west of Ancud, on the coastal road just before you drive into the village. Buen Provecho! Open all year. ◆$$◆ ◆$$$◆

a. Quetalmahue, Chiloé
t. +56 9 8791 9410
i. quetalmahue

Right across from the market in Dalcahue on the east coast of the island, find cute coffee bar and concept store **Casita de Piedra (52)**. We can recommend the tortas and juices at this little haven of tranquility. Open all year. ◆$◆ ◆$$◆

a. Pedro Montt 144, Dalcahue, Chiloé
t. +56 9 9489 9050
fb. Café-artesanías Casita de Piedra

SHOP

◆

Stocking up on food while on Chiloé can best be done at the **Mercado Municipal de Ancud (53)**. Find fresh local produce and handicrafts too. Open all year.

a. 198, Dieciocho 108, Ancud, Chiloé

You might want to complement your travel wardrobe with warm socks, or a hat, blanket, sweater or poncho. The **Feria Artesanal de Dalcahue (54)**, held every Sunday near the Dalcahue canal, offers a colorful sight with

expertly crafted items, most of them made from wool. Try putting your Spanish to practice by chatting to the makers, although the Chilote dialect is muy rapido! Open all year.

a. Pedro Montt 105-138, Dalcahue, Chiloé
t. +56 9 8285 2607

SLEEP

◆

Driving along Carelmapu's costanera you can't miss the sight of bobbing rows of fishing boats and, overlooking them, the colorful **Cabañas Tierra Verde Carelmapu (55)**. Hospitable owner Eduardo is a pioneer in the area, in offering accommodation to tourists. There are ten self-catered and fully equipped cabins, all in different sizes and colors, sleeping from 2 up to 7 people. The cabins are simple but have all you need, and each cabin has its own little lush green garden. Open all year. ◆$◆

a. Calle O'Higgins 785, Carelmapu
t. +56 9 4266 8384
w. tierraverdecarelmapu.cl

Located atop a cliff overlooking Mar Brava Beach, you'll be the first to see the waves arrive if you stay at **Carelmapu Surf B & B (56)**. Run by

local surfer Arturo and his family, they have surf classes on offer, and host the Carelmapu Surf Sisters retreat, offering girls and women surf guiding and outdoor adventures in the area. They have cabins available too. Open all year. ◆$◆ ◆$$◆

a. Camino Vecinal Punta Chocoy, Lote 7, Carelmapu
t. +56 9 9019 4667
fb. Carelmapu Surf B&B

Agroturismo and restaurant **Posada El Encanto (57)** is run by a lovely local couple. They've a cabin sleeping 6 people, or for a small fee you can park your van or pitch your tent on their land for the night (ocean sounds included) and use the restaurant's bathroom. It's a heartwarming place where amazing food's served, including their homegrown fruit, vegetables and herbs. Open all year, during low season making a reservation in advance is advised, so the owners are prepared. ◆$◆

a. Faro Corona Rural 343, Punta Corona, Chiloé
t. +56 9 8330 4884
w. chiloefarocorona.webnode.es

Agroturismo Ballena Azul (58) is located on a quiet part of the

island, close to the penguin colonies of Puñihuil. They've a restaurant and campsite with basic but clean facilities, and the surroundings are breathtaking. Named after the whales that you might be lucky enough to see passing by! You can follow a stunning jungle trail down the cliff to the beach. Open all year. ◆$◆

a. Pumillahue rural s/n, Chiloé
t. +56 9 9558 9878
fb. Agroturismo Ballena Azul

At **Palafito Cucao Lodge (59)** you can sleep in a traditional Palafito stilt house, right on the water's edge. The lodge is located south of the national park, overlooking Lago Cucao and adjoining Lago Huillinco. They've double, twin and triple rooms, and larger family rooms; all are bright, with high ceilings and almost everything the whole place over is made from wood. Guests can use the shared living room and kitchen to hang out and cook at home, or wander along the road to one of several restaurants within walking distance. The breakfast provided at the lodge needs a special mention too - it's absolutely delicious. The big bonus here, however, is spotting birds and sea otters from your window. If you feel like Señor Relax-a-Lot you can book the outdoor wooden hot tub or wander the little wooden walkways to a peaceful terrace. More in the active mood? Take one of the kayaks for a spin around the lake. The lodge offers plenty more adventure tours, like trekking and horse riding, and your hosts will be delighted to share tips for what to do in the area (including giving you directions to a stunning jungle beach nearby). Open all year. ◆$$$◆

a. Cucao, Chiloé
t. +56 9 8403 4728
w. palafitocucaolodge.com

SURF

Remote fishing villages, untouched natural landscapes, ancient cultural heritage and about as empty as you can find line-ups await. Accepting the risk of sounding clichéd; time really does seem to have stood still in this part of the country. While you're traveling back in time in the best of ways, you'll want to bring along your newest, thickest wetsuit. And boots and gloves, and a good hood. It may not be icy like south Patagonia, but the water definitely has a chilly tingle.

VALDIVIA (I)

From a coastal point of view, the gray sand beach of **Mehuín** is where the Los Ríos region begins. The sandbanks formed by the Lingue river estuary provide consistent waves, sometimes powerful and hollow. Up until now, the Mehuín community has

successfully protected this magical place from development and will continue to do so. They've a strong connection to the sea, and the cultural legacy of the Mapuche-Lafkenche is still very much alive. ◆ *All levels/sand/ shower/toilet/restaurant/surf shop/ surf school/easy parking.* ◆

Playa Grande in Niebla is a beautiful beach at the mouth of the Valdivian river estuary. It's not very consistent but is beginner friendly. On good days you can expect some crowds due to its close proximity to the city. ◆ *All levels/ sand/restaurant/easy parking.* ◆

While driving along the coastal road T-352, you might want to check out beautiful **Calfuco** beach. In Mapudungun, Calfu means blue and Co means water, which sums up this spot perfectly. Tread with care, it's also a bird sanctuary. There are no facilities.

Playa Pilolcura, also known as Roca Hueca - hollow stone - is named after the hollowed out rock you'll see at the beach. On good days, expect longboardable waves and a stunning landscape. There are no facilities.

PUCATRIHUE (II)

Puca, as the locals refer to it, is an all-level break in the commune of San Juan de la Costa, in the Los Lagos region. The area is steeped in the culture of the Mapuche-Huilliche (people from the sea). Surfing's relatively fresh here and the locals are a friendly and welcoming bunch - please repay them with the same friendliness and respect. ♦ *All levels/sand and rocks/restaurant/surf school/easy parking.* ♦

CARELMAPU (III)

Playa Mar Brava in Carelmapu is a 10 km long, south-facing beach with good peaks that work best from mid to high tide. There are no facilities. ♦ *Intermediate/sand and rocks/easy parking.* ♦

CHILOÉ (IV)

Like we said in the intro to this chapter, the islanders, Chilotes, have a strong connection to the ocean but riding waves is of more recent years. Respecting the delicate line between an undisclosed paradise and the prospect of exploring the unknown, we strongly advise that you connect with local surfers before setting out on your own search. An all-level, white sand beach can be found west of Ancud at **Guabun beach**. You'll find several peaks to choose from.

SCHOOL RENTAL SHOP

◆

In Mehuín, our favorite place to hang out and check the waves with a coffee is **Escuela de Surf NewenLafken** (**60**). Located right in front of the beach, the school's run by welcoming couple Geo and Ona. You'll not only be treated with sweet pastries but also learn some of their astonishing knowledge about the local environment and surf. Lessons and rental and rental of gear are on offer too. Open all year.

- a. Costanera s/n, Mehuín
- t. +56 9 9150 6319
- i. escuelasurfmehuin

Pancho from **Puihua Pucatrihue** (**61**) offers surf lessons, rentals, and

surf necessities like wax and leashes. Open all year.

- a. Pucatrihue
- t. +56 9 7762 1784
- i. puihua_pucatrihue

Within walking distance from Pucatrihue's surf break, find the wooden shack of **Escuela de Surf Pucatrihue** (**62**). Lessons and rentals are on the menu alongside a little skate ramp and a knowledgeable team. Open all year.

- a. Pucatrihue
- i. pucatrihue_club_de_surf

Passion and a love for the south led Santiago-born Arturo to open up one of the southernmost surf schools in Chile, **Carelmapu Surf** (**63**). You can ask him all and anything about the area (he speaks perfect English). Lessons and rentals available. Beside the surf school he runs a hostel with a great view of Mar Brava beach. Open all year.

- a. Camino Vecinal Punta Chocoy, Lote 7, Carelmapu
- t. +56 9 9019 4667
- i. carelmapusurf

El Secreto Chilote Surf School (**64**) is a mobile surf school, with their office based in Ancud. They'll take you to the best locations depending on conditions. They usually operate from the beaches Mar Brava (Polucue, Ancud), Guabun and Chillimo. Their team also organize surf trips. Open all year (daily in summer, weekends only the rest of the year).

- a. Errazuriz 309, Ancud, Isla de Chiloé
- i. elsecretochilotesurfschool

The ultimate companion for an adventurous outdoor lifestyle

N° 12 Outdoor Explorer

OPINEL
SAVOIE FRANCE

opinel.cl   www.opinel.cl

SEASIDE LOCAL: VICTORIA ANSALDO

◆

Meet Victoria Ansaldo, a young Chilean woman who travels her home country in her classic 1985 VW Kombi T2 named Octavia. Photographing and shooting audiovisual content of the natural beauty of her homeland, she created herself a dream job.

Under the name Octavia Viajando - Octavia travels - Victoria shoots videos and photos to tell stories on her socials and blog. Most scenes depict the mind-boggling beauty of Chile, encounters with wildlife, and local folks and fellow travelers that she meets along the way. Some of her stories tell of withstanding the cold, heat, rain, storms, a mechanical problem with the van, or any van issue. She uses limited means and technical knowledge to her advantage, all the while wearing a winning smile.

"I am an engineer by profession and a photographer by passion and today this is my main job. In 2016 I bought a VW Kombi, which I called Octavia, to restore it and turn it into a vanlife-style mobile home to start touring my country and one day the world. I really love nature, the nomadic life, meeting new people on the road and sharing my travel adventures on my blog. All this, complemented by my truck and photography, allowed me to live life as I always wanted, on the move."

En constante movimiento, as her bio on Instagram reads. What made her decide to embark on such a grand adventure at such a young age?

"When I started the project, I wanted to share the entire process of restoring and converting the van, so I wanted to give it a name. I always thought that this car would be my traveling companion, so I wanted to personify her, coming up with the name Octavia. A name with character, I wanted it to be an inspiring project for other women to dare to fulfill their dreams and get to know the world. When I bought the van I was only 20 years old, I had worked hard to one day buy my own van. As I was still studying, I thought it would be a good idea to start at that moment with this dream that I had in mind, so I could work without rushing on it, so Octavia would be super equipped to travel."

CREATING HER OWN DREAMLIFE

◆

If ever there was an 'aha' moment, a sudden insight or inspiration that made her choose this path, it was the realization that she couldn't wait around for another person to fulfill her dream.

"I have always thought that life is fleeting, just so short that you have to take advantage of it, live it. And my goal in life was to find a job where I would be happy. I never thought that buying the Kombi would lead to this, but here I am, working on my own brand that I created, Octavia Viajando."

Photo: @octaviaviajando

Just blogging about your travels doesn't really pay the bills, so to speak, but Victoria takes blogging and social posting to the next level, venturing into unknown territory, setting goals and sharing her adventures online. Even while pulling off some superhuman feats - like driving her old van through deserts or doing multiple day treks to discover new places, camping out at Tierra del Fuego, spotting foxes, or (what!) pumas - she comes across as the girl next door; an enthusiastic and very approachable person that you'd easily befriend. With incredible skill - plus meticulous preparation, hard work offline and online - Victoria distinguished herself well enough to get noticed by big outdoor brands, like Stanley. She gets to try out all their sturdy tools, cups and flasks as well!

"Creating photographic and audiovisual content for different brands supports me on my trips, I'm so grateful for that. I send them content so they can upload it to their own networks. On my website I also share travel itineraries to get to know Chile: the routes that I have been able to discover."

THE SPARKS OF INSPIRATION

◆

No doubt Victoria's an inspiration to many, but she needs to get her spark from somewhere too. She explains she's a person driven partly by emotions. And the emotions that come up while undertaking an adventurous trip inspire her.

"The route, the different events that help you grow, help you see the bright side of things despite that sometimes they make us feel weak. I try to be inspired by nature, by moments of light to photograph, by other travelers who roam the world."

"Another very important point that inspires me are the messages from the people who follow my journey through social networks, when they tell me their stories, or made the decision to travel in the same way as I do. Seeing that a little spark is generated in others, inspires me even more to continue with this project."

ON SOLO TRAVELING

◆

At some point or other in life we all have, or will face, a moment of Feel the Fear and Do It Anyway. Solo traveling as a young woman, sometimes through tough or hostile territory, Victoria's had her share. They can make up the worst and the best moments in life though…

"When I started out on this journey and knew I was going to travel alone I obviously had some fears. Like having mechanical problems on the road, getting stuck in the car, or being robbed. But I had to face those fears to really know what it was like to travel like this, and I was learning to anticipate risk situations.

I also feared that in the end I might not like it at all, traveling the way I opted for. And all the work I had invested in this project wouldn't adapt to my way of being. But soon enough I realized that it is definitely what I like."

OCEAN LOVE AND THE PERFECTION OF NATURE

◆

We're obviously ocean loving, and the ocean has Victoria's deep respect too.

"I have lived all my life by the sea, every time I could escape to the beach with my dogs or ride a bike I did. On my first road trips with friends who surfed, I accompanied them and I took pictures. Sometimes I tried to learn too, but it was not what I liked the most. Lately, I have gotten much closer to the sea, taking the Advanced PADI diving course which has only increased my love for the sea, seeing it from a different perspective. I am very motivated with the world of diving, I think I found something that adapts a lot to my lifestyle, travel and photography. Giving much value to new places to discover in the world! The ocean and all the life that is in it plays a fundamental role in our lives, that is why we must take care of it."

What Victoria likes most about traveling is the freedom. The freedom to be able to decide how much time you want to spend in a certain place and who with.

"To go out and explore nature, do a trekking and make photos, no matter the weather. I think it's a very good way to get closer to nature, and you realize that you don't need much to be happy in life. I also really like meeting new people and hearing their travel stories, learning what it's like to live in other places, that sort of thing. And without a doubt, getting to know new places, places that leave an imprint of the perfect natural creation."

Her favorite places in Chile are in the far reaches of the country:

"Up north it's the mountain range in the Atacama region, it is different from San Pedro de Atacama - the route of the six thousand, where there are large mountains and volcanoes over 6 thousand meters above sea level. The landscapes are similar but still less explored, you do not meet many people there, it is immense and beautiful. In the south, I am fascinated with Patagonia, the Carretera Austral, Torres del Paine, Puelo River and the unexplored fjords of Patagonia."

FINDING BALANCE
◆

After a few years on her own, Victoria is now occasionally accompanied by friends or family on her travels, when their work or schedule allows. But in order to find a good balance, she's not constantly on the road.

"I try to combine my life on the road with life in my hometown Viña del Mar, working on new projects and preparing group trips. After 6 months on the move, either in my van or on work trips, I return for a few months to work on other projects, or prep for a new trip. In my day-to-day life I usually find myself creating, working on photography projects, writing blog articles, figuring out new ideas and travel plans. Traveling life is intense, that's why sometimes I take breaks at home, my base camp, haha. I need to bring some order in all the information and be able to transmit and share all the adventures and newly discovered places. And also to work on job proposals for new brands that wish to support me!"

Some final wise words and wishes from a well-traveled young lady?

"The message that I always share to the people that read about my travel adventures is that we should never lose the power to marvel at simple things. That way we enjoy life more. Smile more, look for the good side of things and take the learning it leaves us with, I am sure that a world where collaboration is above personal interest, will be better. And above all, I believe that if we have a dream, we have to try and go for it, and focus all our energies on that goal to achieve it."

◆

Curious about all these places, Victoria's travels, lifestyle, blogs, the places she's been or is going to, or maybe want to join one of her adventurous group trips? Find out more:
w. octaviaviajando.com / **i.** octaviaviajando / **fb.** Octavia Viajando

◆

BALANCING POSE: NATARAJASANA

◆

Dancer's Pose

Balance, grace, focus.

This challenging pose works on hidden muscles within your hips and pelvis which stabilize the spine, doing wonders for your posture.

Benefits:
Improves coordination and balance, stretches psoas muscles (hip flexors), strengthens legs and core, opens shoulders and chest, and boosts your energy.

How:
Stand with your feet shoulder-width apart. Shift your weight onto your right leg as you find a point to focus on in front of you. Bend the left knee, bringing your left foot up behind towards your left buttock. Now reach with your left hand for your inner left foot or ankle, as you raise your right arm straight out ahead of you. Maybe stay here to ease into it slowly, rolling the shoulders back, finding your balance and stretching the quad muscle of your left leg. Then push your left foot into your left hand to create a backbend and simultaneously reach your right hand forward. Keep gazing forward and keep lifting the chest. Think 'heart forward.' Ground through your right foot and breathe. Try coming out of the pose with control, then change sides.

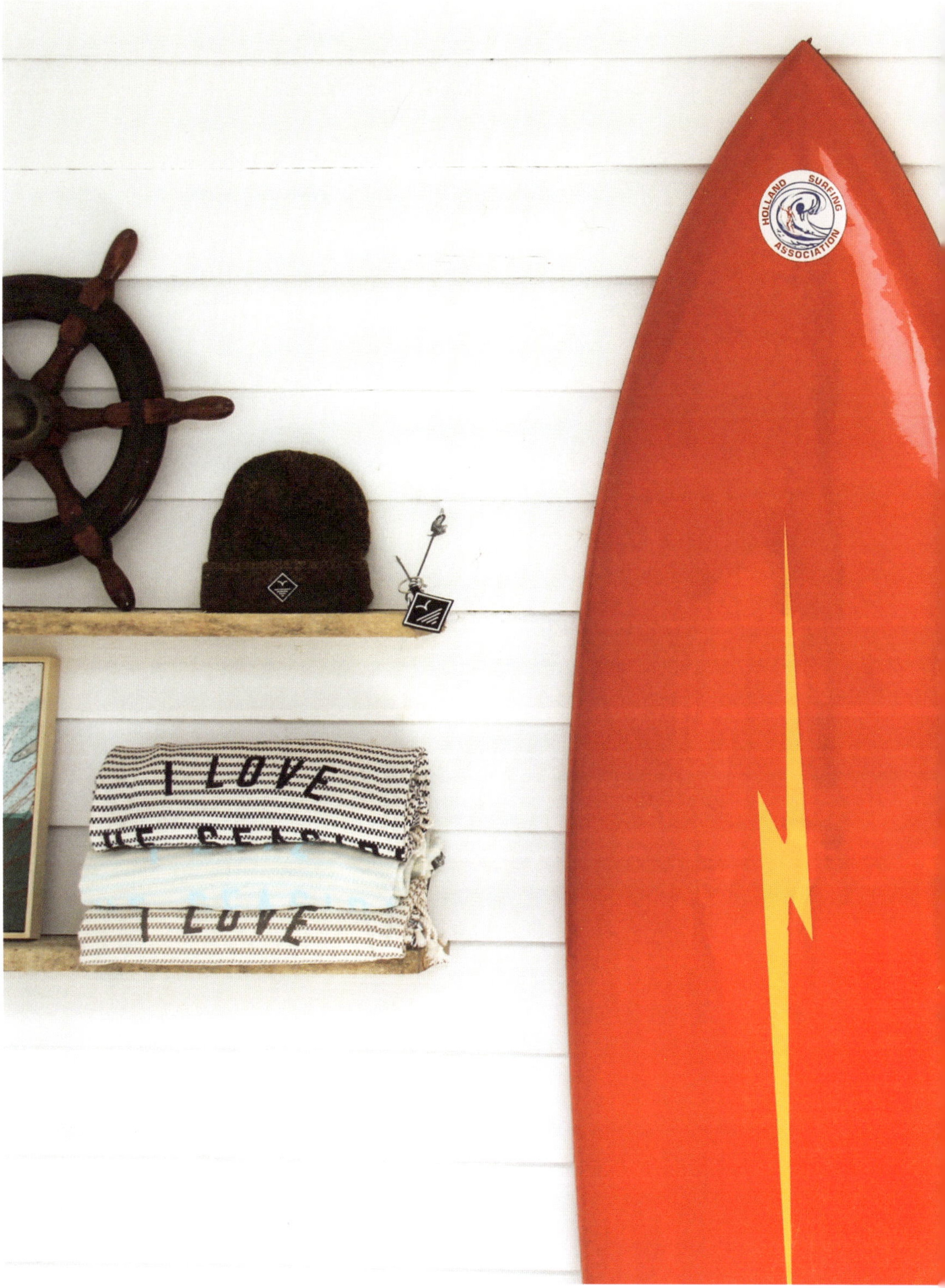
HOLLAND SURFING ASSOCIATION
I LOVE
I LOVE

THERE'S MORE I LOVE THE SEASIDE!

*Check out our online shop for I Love the Seaside travel essentials.
We're talking sexy Seaside enamel mugs, super thermos flasks, snuggly soft beach towels, keyrings, lanyards, car fresheners, cozy beanies and...
we're adding more all the time, go see for yourself!*

iloveteheseaside.com/shop

THANK YOU!

Here we go again! After yet another adventure, we bring you the brand spanking new, first edition of our I Love the Seaside Surf and Travel Guide to Chile. Made with lots of love, and the indispensable help of many. With our very first best-selling Southwest Europe edition in 2016 we set things in motion; inspiring travelers, and a continuation of creating seaside guides. We can't thank you enough, dear readers, supporters and partners, that we can do just so! We hope to meet you, either in a next edition or on social media (#iloveseaside #surfandtravelguide), but preferably in the ocean. Let us know you're out there, share your story, photo or wave. Stay stoked!

Big up, cheers and thank you to all Seaside friends and family for your faith. And, of course, all welcoming Chilean locals who shared ins and outs, Yeti Campers, Tribu, SurfEars, Opinel, Stanley, Victoria Ansaldo (Octavia Viajando), Kris Cabezas, Lorena Fica, Álvaro Cáceres and Maikel Kersbergen..

I Love the Seaside
Wassenaarsestraat 110
2586 AR Scheveningen
The Netherlands

t.   +31 6 53 178 129
e.   info@iloveseaside.com
w. iloveseaside.com
ig. iloveseaside
fb. iloveseaside

ISBN 978 90 831 7672 7
NUR 515
First edition, 2024

Printed in the EU by Real Concepts,
w. realconcepts.nl
Paper from responsible sources.
Printed with vegetable oil-based ink.

Concept & text: zee-inkt.nl
Design and art-direction: dimrooker.com
Copyediting: gailbennie.com
Merchandise: sourxing.com

Photography:
Vicente Gracia, Marte Louwes, Maikel Kersbergen, Victoria Ansaldo (Octavia Viajando)

Cover photo:
Victoria Ansaldo (w. octaviaviajando.com)

Want to sell our beautiful guides in your shop?
e. gj@iloveseaside.com

MAURICIO ROVIRA

IN LOVING MEMORY OF MAURICIO ROVIRA
INSPIRATION AND TRAVELER PUR SANG
'UN ABRAZO AL CIELO TATA'

All rights reserved.
No part of this guide (or publication) may be reproduced in any forms or by any means, stored in a retrieval system, or transmitted, in any form or by any means, electronic, graphic, photocopying, mechanical, recording, or otherwise without the permission of the publishers and copyright owners.

I Love the Seaside and the I Love the Seaside logo are a registered trademark of I Love the Seaside.

Feedback.
This guide has been compiled with the utmost care and attention to detail, however, details may change. Travelers should be aware that recommended providers and services may move, alter provisions or services, prices or opening times.

Having said that, we'd love your help! Please let us know about your experiences, share your knowledge, opinions, tips and insights - email us: info@iloveseaside.com

Independent.
To clarify, we would like to assure you that none of the recommendations listed in our guide have paid by any means for entry in this guide.

I Love the Seaside is not liable for any injury or inconvenience however caused, or any inaccuracies in the text.

Please note.
Maps are solely indicators of locations, they are not intended to be used as road maps.
© OpenStreetMap.org

ABOUT US

ALEXANDRA GOSSINK

CO-WRITER, RESEARCH & CONCEPT

Never really needs a break from traveling as a journalist, writing stories, surfing and walking the dogs. Likes her life to be healthy and happy.

i. alexandra.gossink

GEERT-JAN MIDDELKOOP

PRODUCTION, RESEARCH & CONCEPT

Seaside explorer since childhood. Manages to do a lot of trade and business between sessions. When he's not on a surf trip in his campervan, he's planning one.

i. geertjan.middelkoop

DIM ROOKER

GRAPHIC DESIGNER, ART-DIRECTION & CONCEPT

Gets his inspiration from the ocean. Besides designing and working on concepts for brands, books and websites, he creates his own art and loves to take his family on van-adventures.

i. dimrooker

VICENTE GRACIA

CHILE EXPLORER, RESEARCH & PHOTOS

Born and raised in Chile, loves adventures and boards; whether skate, surf, kite or snow. But if he had to choose, he'd pick the ocean, since it's his way of meditation.

i. v.gracia10

MARTE LOUWES

CHILE EXPLORER, RESEARCH, PHOTOS & YOGA POSES

Amsterdam based, loves the beach and finds her peace on the yoga mat. She likes to discover new perspectives, collect adventures and insights, and share any knowledge she's gathered.

i. marte_onthemat

GAIL BENNIE

CO-WRITER, RESEARCH, PROOFREADER & COPYEDITOR

Ocean-loving wordbird longboarder, currently on a stopover in Jersey, Channel Islands. Never far from the sea, ILtS family member from the very start.

i. gailbennie

#ILOVETHESEASIDE

Share your I Love the Seaside stories! Check our website to be inspired about your future travels, find new places to surf, shop, eat, drink or hang out. Buy your travel essentials or even book your next holiday...

facebook.com/ilovetheseaside
instagram.com/ilovetheseaside

ilovetheseaside.com